Puss in Books

A Collection of
Great Cat Quotations

PUSS IN BOOKS

Compiled and Edited by

Maria Polushkin Robbins

THE ECCO PRESS

THE ECCO PRESS
100 West Broad Street
Hopewell, New Jersey 08525

Published simultaneously in Canada by
Penguin Books Canada Ltd., Ontario
Printed in the United States of America

Library of Congress Cataloging-in-Publication Data

Puss in books / compiled and edited by Maria Polushkin Robbins. —
1st Ecco ed.
p.   cm
Includes index
ISBN 0-88001-588-8
1. Cats—Quotations, maxims, etc.   I. Polushkin, Maria.
PN6084.C23P87   1998
636.8—dc21   97-22656

Designed by Eve L. Kirch
The text of this book is set in Century Expanded

9   8   7   6   5   4   3   2   1

FIRST ECCO EDITION 1998

To Lucy, Sammy, Tess, Mikey, Sufi, Pi, Kid, Kisya, Chablis, Vaska, Flower, Chub-Chub, Kitty, Evita, O.J. and all the other great cats who have crossed my path.

CONTENTS

INTRODUCTION

As I hope this anthology will make clear, there is not much that can be said about those of the feline purrsuasion that hasn't already been set in print. Though never truly domesticated, cats have been such fascinating companions to mankind for so many centuries as to have elicited by now a very wide range of comment indeed.

Passionate feelings, of course, tend to predominate, since the cat is a subject about which hardly anyone is neutral. It may be true that most of the more amusing things that have been said about cats have been said by curmudgeons and cat haters, but cat lovers, too, are given (as they must be) to whimsy and to good (if occasionally rueful) humor. It is only their more zealous brethren, the Cat Fanciers, and their yet even more far-gone kin, the Cat Nuts, who can on occasion seem a bit humorless.

People's reactions to cats being as varied and various as cats themselves, it's not possible to accurately summarize what you'll find on these pages. Some may feel that dogs are treated unfairly, but I hasten to say that if they are disparaged, it is not in their own right, but merely insofar as they are compared with cats.

Cats are smarter than dogs. You can't get eight
cats to pull a sled through snow.

—JEFF VALDEZ

By and large, people who enjoy teaching animals to roll over will find themselves happier
with a dog.

—BARBARA HOLLAND

Some apologize for the cat's ferocity with small scurrying
things, some deny it, some see it for what it undoubtedly is:
Nature just being Herself. Nevertheless, the utility of cats
as regards pest control has been acknowledged by a considerable number of authors:

Let take a cat, and foster him well with milk
And tender flesh, and make his couch of silk,
And let him see a mouse go by the wall,
Anon he waveth milk, and flesh, and all,
And every dainty which is in that house,
Such appetite hath he to eat a mouse.

—CHAUCER

Much has also been made of their legendary ability to
land on their feet (a talent sometimes overestimated by curious children, with tragic results).

> Throw a cat over a house and it will land on its feet.
>
> —ENGLISH PROVERB

The beauty, grace, intelligence, and self-possession of cats are all mentioned so often as to amount to a consensus, and one immutable law is almost universally recognized. In its simplest formulation the law states that you cannot bend a cat to the human will.

> If a cat can detect no self-advantage in what it is being told to do, it says the hell with it, and, if pressure is brought to bear, it will grow increasingly surly and irritable to the point where it is hopeless to continue.
>
> —JOHN D. MACDONALD

Dan Greenburg, perhaps, sums it up best. "There is," he has noted, "no way of talking about cats that enables one to come off as a sane person."

In Praise of Cats

If a man could be crossed with the cat, it would improve man but deteriorate the cat. —MARK TWAIN

Two things are aesthetically perfect in the world—the clock and the cat. —EMILE-AUGUST CHARTIER

The cat, in dignity and independence, is very much like the human animal should be but isn't. Perhaps that's my strongest reason for choosing the cat as a subject for the human animal to watch: some of the cat's dignity and independence may rub off on the watcher. —PAUL COREY

With the qualities of cleanliness, discretion, affection, patience, dignity, and courage that cats have, how many of us, I ask you, would be capable of being cats?
—FERNAND MÉRY

*Way down deep, we're all
motivated by the same urges.
Cats have the courage to live
by them.*

—Jim Davis

The cat is witty, he has nerve, he knows how to do precisely the right thing at the right moment. He is impulsive and facetious and appreciates the value of a well-turned pleasantry. He extricates himself from the most difficult situations by a little pirouette. To how many timid and hesitating persons could he give useful lessons. I have never seen him embarrassed. With an astounding promptitude he chooses instantly between two solutions of a problem, not merely that which is better from his point of view and in conformity with his interests, but also that which is elegant and gracious. —Jules Henri Poincaré

Stately, kindly, lordly friend,
Condescend
Here to sit by me, and turn
Glorious eyes that smile and burn,
Golden eyes, love's lustrous meed,
On the golden page I read.

All your wondrous wealth of hair,
Dark and fair,
Silken-shaggy, soft and bright
As the clouds and beams of night,
Pays my reverent hand's caress
Back with friendlier gentleness.

—ALGERNON SWINBURNE

A cat has absolute emotional honesty: human beings, for one reason or another, may hide their feelings, but a cat does not.　　　　　—ERNEST HEMINGWAY

The cat is utterly sincere.　　　　　—FERNAND MÉRY

O cat of ashen coat! To the uninitiated you look like every other gray cat on earth, lazy, oblivious, morose, somewhat listless, neuter, bored ... but I know you to be wildly tender, and whimsical, jealous to the point of starving yourself, talkative, paradoxically awkward, and, on occasion, as tough as a young mastiff.　　　　　—COLETTE

A cat improves the garden wall in sunshine, and the hearth in foul weather.
—Judith Merkle Riley

There is not a man living who knows better than I that the four charms of a cat lie in its closed eyes, its long and lovely hair, its silence and even its affected love.
—Hilaire Belloc

There is nothing sweeter than his peace when at
    rest.
For there is nothing brisker than his life when
    in motion.

                   —CHRISTOPHER SMART

*Thou art the Great Cat, the avenger of
the Gods, and the judge of words, and the
president of the sovereign chiefs and the
governor of the holy Circle; thou art
indeed . . . the Great Cat.*

    —INSCRIPTION ON THE ROYAL TOMBS AT THEBES

You see the beauty of the world
Through eyes of unalloyed content,
And in my study chair upcurled,
Move me to pensive wonderment.

I wish I knew your trick of thought,
The perfect balance of your ways;
They seem an inspiration, caught
From other laws in older days.

                   —ANONYMOUS

For push of nose, for perseverance, there is nothing to beat a cat.
—EMILY CARR

As to Sagacity, I should say that his judgment respecting the warmest place and the softest cushion in a room is infallible, his punctuality at meal times is admirable, and his pertinacity in jumping on people's shoulders till they give him some of the best of what is going, indicates great firmness.
—THOMAS HENRY HUXLEY

Some people say that cats are sneaky, evil, and cruel. True, and they have many other fine qualities as well.
—MISSY DIZICK

Beautiful Cats

Cats are *always* elegant. —JOHN WEITZ

I will admit to feeling exceedingly proud when any cat has singled me out for notice; for, of course, every cat is really the most beautiful woman in the room. That is part of their deadly fascination. —E. V. LUCAS

Oh cat; I'd say, or pray: be-oootiful cat! Delicious cat! Exquisite cat! Satiny cat! Cat like a soft owl, cat with paws like moths, jewelled cat, miraculous cat! Cat, cat, cat, cat. —DORIS LESSING

And let me touch those curving claws of yellow ivory, and grasp the tail that like a monstrous asp coils round your heavy velvet paws. —OSCAR WILDE

A cat's rage is beautiful, burning
with pure cat flame, all its hair
standing up and crackling blue sparks,
eyes blazing and sputtering.

—WILLIAM S. BURROUGHS

Cats are living adornments.   —EDWIN LENT

Balanchine has trained his cat to perform brilliant *jetés* and *tours en l'air;* he says that at last he has a body worth choreographing for.   —BERNARD TAPER

C was a lovely Pussy Cat;
its eyes were large & pale;
And on its back it had some stripes,
and several on his tail.

—EDWARD LEAR

For I am possessed of a cat, surpassing in beauty,
from whom I take occasion to bless Almighty God.

—CHRISTOPHER SMART

Cats, like women, should be respected as individuals rather than admired as decoration, but there's no harm, given a choice, in taking up with a strikingly attractive specimen of either. —BARBARA HOLLAND

I love cats because they are so beautiful aesthetically. They are like sculpture walking around the house.

—WANDA TOSCANINI HOROWITZ

I saw the most beautiful cat today. It was sitting by the side of the road, its two front feet neatly and graciously together. Then it gravely swished around its tail to completely encircle itself. It was so *fit* and beautifully neat, that gesture, and so self-satisfied—so complacent.

—ANNE MORROW LINDBERGH

Like a graceful vase, a cat, even when motionless, seems to flow. —GEORGE F. WILL

It is odd that, notwithstanding the extreme beauty of cats, their elegance of motion, the variety and intensity of their colour, they should be so little painted by considerable artists. —Philip Gilbert Hamerton

There's no need for a piece of sculpture in a home that has a cat. —Wesley Bates

They're the most graceful, sinuous, sexy, truly sensuous creatures in the world. —Carol Lawrence

What cat was ever awkward or clumsy? Whether in play or in earnest, cats are the very embodiment of elegance. —Charles H. Ross

Aristocratic Cats

Among animals, cats are the top-hatted, frock-coated statesmen going about their affairs at their own pace.
—ROBERT STEARNS

Webster was very large and very black and very composed. He conveyed the impression of being a cat of deep reserves. Descendant of a long line of ecclesiastical ancestors who had conducted their decorous courtships beneath the shadow of cathedrals and on the back walls of bishops' palaces, he had that exquisite poise which one sees in high dignitaries of the Church. His eyes were clear and steady, and seemed to pierce to the very roots of the young man's soul, filling him with a sense of guilt.
—P. G. WODEHOUSE

The cat is truly aristocratic in type and origin.
—ALEXANDRE DUMAS

Monty was an imperious cat, a cat who lived through the bombs on London, who had lived, for a cat, a glamorous life, who was used to being hailed by the crowds on Boat Race day when he sat in the window of our home overlooking the finishing post, wearing a light blue ribbon around his neck. Monty, with his beautiful dark ginger stripes and white shirt front, and a haughty face, was an aristocrat of cats. And I never expected to see any cat like him again.

— Derek Tangye

A cat may look on a king.

— John Heywood

But a king is forever a king; Napoleon upon Elba was not more imperious toward his staff and his guardians than is a

Persian cat suddenly deposited in a milieu wholly foreign to him and no less insistent that, though he be living in exile, his royal prerogatives should be granted him. Nor will mere possession of his earthly body by his captor guarantee possession of the proud creature's soul.

—ROGERS E. M. WHITAKER

It is easy to understand why the rabble dislike cats. A cat is beautiful; it suggests ideas of luxury, cleanliness, voluptuous pleasures.

—CHARLES BAUDELAIRE

Socks Clinton, unlike Madonna, did absolutely nothing to attract the world's attention. Furthermore, he will continue to do absolutely nothing. If guests at the White House hope to see him, he'll probably hide. Anyone who expects him to be cute on command has never met a cat.

Despite his adoptive family's determined efforts to shield him from the press, Socks Clinton will stay famous all the time Chelsea Clinton's father is in office. Nonetheless, his will remain a cat's life: snoozing followed by eating followed by snoozing followed by pushing corks across the kitchen floor. At times he may be impelled to claw the leg of a chair. But he will never have to claw his way to the top.

—*NEW YORK TIMES* EDITORIAL

Caresses were agreeable to her, but she responded to them with great reserve, and only to those of people whom she favored with her esteem, which it was not easy to gain. She liked luxury, and it was always in the newest armchair or on the piece of furniture best calculated to show off her swan-like beauty, that she was to be found. Her toilette took an immense time. She would carefully smooth her entire coat every morning, and wash her face with her paw, and every hair on her body shone like new silver when brushed by her pink tongue. If anyone touched her she would immediately efface all traces of contact, for she could not endure being ruffled. Her elegance and distinction gave one an idea of aristocratic birth, and among her own kind she must have been at least a duchess. She had a passion for scents. She would plunge her nose into bouquets, and nibble at a perfumed handkerchief with little paroxysms of delight. She would walk about on the dressing-table sniffling the stoppers of the scent-bottles, and she would have loved to use the violet powder if she had been allowed.

Such was Seraphita, and never was a cat more worthy of a poetic name.   —Théophile Gautier

Cats are *always* elegant. They know that the secret of elegance is a combination of several components: *fear*— affection to be given grudgingly and withdrawn on whim;

suspicion—to create mystery; and *security*—acquired from the ability to run like hell. Cats are also superbly dressed in great colors and fabrics: each possesses one supremely simple outfit which never wears out.   —JOHN WEITZ

Found Cats

It's just an old alley cat that has followed us all the way home. It hasn't a star on its forehead, or a silky satiny coat. No proud tiger stripes, no dainty tread, no elegant velvet throat. It's a splotchy, blotchy city cat, not a pretty cat, a rough little bag of old bones. 'Beauty,' we shall call you. 'Beauty,' come in. —EVE MERRIAM

Quite a little puss, a grey kitten three or four months old, striped like a tiger, besides being spotted, his tail ring-streaked like a panther's, belly and muzzle white, and the end of his nose quite pink. He made his appearance one morning—Heaven alone knows where he sprang from!—a pitiable sight, lean and wretched looking. Within a very short time he recovered, and for the past fortnight has been my most devoted companion. —PIERRE LOTI

I said that the only cat I would have again had to be black, had to come to the cottage in a storm, and that we would never be able to trace the home it came from. True I had al-

ways believed in the luck of black cats even in my most vir-
ulent anti-cat period. But it seemed to be expecting too
much for such conditions ever to be realised.

—DEREK TANGYE

It is always diverting to find something ... but to find a cat:
that is unheard of! For you must agree with me that ...
even though it belongs to us now, it remains somehow
apart, outside, and thus we always have:

life + a cat

Which, I can assure you, adds up to an incalculable sum.

—RAINER MARIA RILKE

Every House Should Have One

For every house is incompleat without him, and a blessing
is lacking in the spirit.   —CHRISTOPHER SMART

> No home should be without the Cat
> Aspeshly where there's Mouses
> It never goes away, the Cat,
> But stays jest where the house is.
>   —ANTHONY HENDERSON EUWER

*Two cats can live as cheaply
as one, and their owner has
twice as much fun.*
                    —LLOYD ALEXANDER

A house without either a cat or a dog is the house of a scoundrel. —PORTUGUESE PROVERB

American families are smaller than they once were. So they simply replaced Sis with a cat. —KATHLEEN FURY

Let your boat of life be light, packed with only what you need—a homely home and simple pleasures, one or two friends, worth the name, someone to love and someone to love you, a cat, a dog, and a pipe or two, enough to eat and enough to wear; and a little more than enough to drink; for thirst is a dangerous thing. —JEROME K. JEROME

Never quite fulfilled is the household without a cat or two. —ROGERS E. M. WHITAKER

Since each of us is blessed with only one life, why not live it with a cat? —ROBERT STEARNS

Books and cats and fair-haired little girls make the best furnishing for a room. —FRENCH PROVERB

I cannot exist without a cat.

—Peggy Bacon

Cat *n.* A soft indestructible automaton provided by nature to be kicked when things go wrong in the domestic circle.

—Ambrose Bierce

Keeping a Cat

Ye shall not possess any beast, my dear sisters, except only a cat. —*ANCRENE RIWLE* ("NUN'S RULE," c.1200)

Some men are born to cats, others have cats thrust upon them. —GILBERT MILLSTEIN

If we have a decent sort of cat to begin with, and have always treated it courteously, and aren't cursed with meddling, bullying natures, it's a pleasure to let it do as it pleases. With children, this would be wicked and irresponsible, so raising children involves a lot of effort and friction. They need to be taught how to tie their shoes and multiply fractions, they need to be punished for pocketing candy in the grocery store, they need to be washed and combed and forced to clean up their rooms and say please and thank you.

A cat is our relief and our reward. —BARBARA HOLLAND

I have myself found, the result of many years' enquiry and study, that all people who keep cats ... do not suffer from those petty ailments which all flesh is heir to.

—Louis Wain

The best exercise for a cat is another cat.
—Jo and Paul Loeb

You always ought to have tom cats arranged, you know—it makes 'em more companionable.   —Noel Coward

To keep a cat at home, butter its feet.   —Proverb

The way to keep a cat is to try to chase it away.
—Ed Howe

Let a cat do what a cat's got to do—or live to regret it.
—*New York Times* editorial

Ask anyone who has ever loved a cat. There is no sound more deep, more all-enveloping than the silence of a sick cat. The emptiness, the hollowness, reaches out and fills the air of a house while the animal sits in the middle, folded into itself, unreachable, unresponding.   —Dr. Louis J. Camuti

Let us admit that "Cat Lover" hardly serves: "Lover" implies equality. No, are we not Cat Servants, are we not, happy in our work, with a master the hem of whose garment is in unending need of touching. And not just the hem—the whole furry garment!   —Malachi McCormick

By associating with the cat, one only risks becoming richer.

—Colette

Happy owner, happy cat. Indifferent owner, reclusive cat.
—Chinese proverb

I don't mind a cat, in its place. But its place is not in the middle of my back at 4 a.m.   —Maynard Good Stoddard

The cat is a guest and not a plaything.
                              —COLETTE

I have (and long shall have) a white, great,
    nimble cat.
A king upon a mouse, a strong foe to the rat.
                        —SIR PHILIP SIDNEY

The cat in the abstract—a beautiful, graceful, athletic animal. A cat, yours, is a soiled litter box, hair on the chrome
coffee table, and something you have to feed and take into
account if you travel. A cat, like any animal, is a commit-
ment.
                              —ROGER A. CARAS

It is as easy to hold quicksilver between your finger and thumb as to keep a cat who means to escape.

—ANDREW LANG

Owning a cat, especially from kittenhood, is a lot like having a child. You feed him, do your best to educate him, talk to him as if he understands you—and, in exchange, you want him to love you. He can drive you mad with his independence. He can, just a surely as a child, create a tremendous desire to protect him from anything bad. He is small, vulnerable, wonderful to hold—when he lets you. And he throws up on just about the same regular schedule.

—PETER GETHERS

"Anyway, I want a cat," she said. "I want a cat. I want a cat now. If I can't have long hair or any fun, I can have a cat."

—ERNEST HEMINGWAY

Feeding the Cat

A plate is distasteful to a cat, a newspaper still worse; they like to eat sticky pieces of meat sitting on a cushioned chair or a nice Persian rug. —MARGARET BENSON

My cat is an elegant eater
of garbage, meat and cream.
—JOHN INGLIS HALL

If you say "Hallelujah" to a cat, it will excite no fixed set of fibres in connection with any other set and the cat will exhibit none of the phenomena of consciousness. But if you say "Me-e-at," the cat will be there in a moment.
—SAMUEL BUTLER

A cat in distress,
Nothing more, nor less;
Good folks, I must faithfully tell ye,
As I am a sinner,

It waits for some dinner,
To stuff out its own little belly.
—PERCY BYSSHE SHELLEY

Each evening Lucio brought home a pint of milk for her
supper and breakfast: Nitchevo sat quietly waiting on her
haunches while he poured it into the cracked saucer bor-
rowed from the landlady and set it on the floor beside the
bed. Then he lay down on the bed, expectantly watching,
while Nitchevo came slowly forward to the pale blue saucer.
She looked up at him once—slowly—with her unflickering
yellow eyes before she started to eat, and then she gracefully lowered her small chin to the saucer's edge, the red
satin tip of tongue protruded and the room was filled with
the sweet, faint music of her gently lapping.
—TENNESSEE WILLIAMS

Before a Cat will condescend
To treat you as a trusted friend,
Some little token of esteem
Is needed, like a dish of cream.
—T. S. ELIOT

Pure herring oil is the Port Wine of English Cats.

—Honoré de Balzac

Never ask a hungry cat whether he loves you for yourself alone.   —Dr. Louis J. Camuti

What cat's averse to fish?   —Thomas Gray

Naming a Cat

They say the test of this is whether a man can write an inscription. I say, "Can he name a kitten?" And by this test I am condemned, for I cannot.   —SAMUEL BUTLER

Alfred de Musset
Used to call his cat Pusset.
His accent was affected.
That was only to be expected.
                                  —MAURICE EVAN HARE

[My cats] died early—on account of being so overweighted with their names, it was thought—"Sour Mash," "Apollinaris," "Zoroaster," "Blatherskite," ... names given them, not in an unfriendly spirit, but merely to practice the children in large and difficult styles of pronunciation. It was a very happy idea—I mean, for the children. —MARK TWAIN

One is called Charles, originally Prince Charlie, not after the present holder of that title, but after earlier romantic princes, for he is a dashing and handsome tabby who knows how to present himself. . . . The other cat, the older brother, with the character of one, has a full ceremonial name, bestowed when he first left kittenhood and his qualities had become evident. We called him General Pinknose the Third, paying tribute, and perhaps reminding ourselves that even the best looked-after cat is going to leave you.

—Doris Lessing

A cat who dislikes his name can—and I am reliably informed, often does—go through his entire lifetime without ever, even by a careless mistake, acknowledging that he has ever heard it before, let alone recognizing, in any perceptible manner known to humankind, that it could in any way have any possible connection with him.

—Cleveland Amory

Do our cats name us? My former husband swore that Humphrey and Dolly and Bean Blossom called me The Big Hamburger.   —Eleanora Walker

Cats must have three names—an everyday name, such as Peter; a more particular, dignified name, such as Quaxo, Bombalurina, or Jellylorum; and, thirdly, the name the cat thinks up for himself, his deep and inscrutable singular Name.

—T. S. Eliot

I called my cat William because no shorter name fits the dignity of his character. Poor old man, he has fits now, so I call him Fitz-William.   —Josh Billings

I have a cat now who thinks he's a dog—you can see it in the way he sits, the way he thinks—but that's all right with me. We have two cats: Ambrosia and James Taylor. We got them as kittens from a girl who was giving them away in front of a supermarket, and as time went by we found out that James Taylor was a girl and Ambrosia was a boy. So now we call them Amberson and Tata. Amberson is the one who thinks he's a dog. He doesn't bark, though, he just purrs.   —George Booth

Our cat had been called various names, but none of them stuck. Melissa and Franny; Marilyn and Sappho; Circe and Ayesha and Suzette. But in conversation, in love talk, she miaowed and purred and throated in response to the long-drawn-out syllables of adjectives—beeeooooti-ful, delicious puss.   —Doris Lessing

If you have been named after a human being of artistic note, run away from home. It is unthinkable that even an

animal should be obliged to share quarters with anyone who
calls a cat Ford Madox Ford. —FRAN LEBOWITZ

*Our old cat has kittens three,
And what do you think their names
    shall be?
Pepper-pot, Sootkins, Scratch-away—
    there!
Was there ever a kitten with these to
    compare?
And we call their old mother, now, what
    do you think?
Tabitha Long-Claws Tiddley-Wink!*
                        —THOMAS HOOD

The first appearance of the domesticated Cat in Egypt is said by some authorities to have been approximately 2500 B.C., and an effigy dating about two centuries later, which was discovered at Beni Hassan, reveals that it was known by the name *Mait*, the feminine form of *Mau*, a word supposed to have been derived from the sound of mewing. The Chinese did not domesticate the Cat until about A.D. 200-400, but a similar thought seems to have inspired their name for it, which was *Mao*, or *Miu*. The Cat's call is expressive of herself, and it has been suggested that the French synonyms of Minette, Minousse, Mimi, etc., and the German Miez, or Mieze-Katze, are also imitations of its sound.   —W. Oldfield Howey

The naming of cats is an almost infallible guide to the degree of affection bestowed on a cat. Perhaps not affection so much as true appreciation of feline character. You may be reasonably sure when you meet a cat called Ginger or merely Puss that his or her owner has insufficient respect for his cat. Such plebeian and unimaginative names are not given to cats by true cat-lovers.   —Michael Joseph

We've got a cat called Ben Hur. We called it Ben till it had kittens.   —Sally Poplin

You get your cat and you call him Thomas or George, as the case may be. So far, so good. Then one morning you wake up and find six kittens in the hat-box and you have to re-open the matter, approaching it from an entirely different angle. —P. G. WODEHOUSE

Working Cats

It is, of course, totally pointless to call a cat when it is intent on the chase. They are deaf to the interruptive nonsense of humans. They are on cat business, totally serious and involved. —JOHN D. MACDONALD

A cat must either have beauty or breeding, or it must have a profession. —MARGARET BENSEN

We had a cat named Minette Mimosa who came with our first Paris apartment. A rather scruffy French maid came with it as well, but we got rid of her. On our first evening in the apartment we were having dinner in our Louis XVI dining salon when three mice appeared. We brought in Minette, who caught them and ate all three in three minutes. We both adored her. —JULIA CHILD

A harmless necessary cat. —WILLIAM SHAKESPEARE

*H*er *function is to sit and be admired.*

—Georgina Strickland Gates

If anyone should steal or kill the Cat that guarded the Prince's granary, he was either to forfeit a milch ewe, her fleece, and lamb, or as much wheat as, when poured on the Cat suspended by its tail (its head touching the floor) would form a heap high enough to cover the tip of the former.   —*A General History of Quadrupeds*

> On some grave business, soft and slow
> Along the garden paths you go
> With bold and burning eyes,
> Or stand with twitching tail to mark
> What starts and rustles in the dark
> Among the peonies.

—A. C. Benson

Cat and Mouse

Yellow cat, black cat, as long as it catches mice, it is a good cat.   —DENG XIAOPING

She sits composedly sentinel, with paws tucked under her, a good part of her days at present, by some ridiculous little hole, the possible entry of a mouse.

—HENRY DAVID THOREAU

> Love to eat them mousies
> Mousies what I love to eat
> Bite they little heads off
> Nibble on they tiny feet.
>
> —B. KLIBAN

Show me a good mouser and I'll show you a cat with bad breath.   —JIM DAVIS

A cat in gloves catches no mice.   —BENJAMIN FRANKLIN

A mouse in the paws is worth two in the pantry.

—LOUIS WAIN

C was Papa's gray Cat,
Who caught a squeaky Mouse;
She pulled him by his twirly tail
All about the house.

—EDWARD LEAR

Did you hear about the cat who ate cheese and waited by
the mouse hole with baited breath?   —ANONYMOUS

For when he takes his prey he plays with it to give it a
    chance.
For one mouse in seven escapes by his dallying.

—CHRISTOPHER SMART

How do you spell mousetrap in three letters?   —RIDDLE

*It is better to feed one cat than many
mice.*

—NORWEGIAN PROVERB

Let take a cat, and foster him well with milk
And tender flesh, and make his couch of silk,
And let him see a mouse go by the wall,
Anon he waveth milk, and flesh, and all,
And every dainty which is in that house,
Such appetite hath he to eat a mouse.

—CHAUCER

Mice amused him, but he usually considered them too small
game to be taken seriously; I have seen him play for an
hour with a mouse and then let him go with a royal conde-
scension.   —CHARLES DUDLEY WARNER

Mr. Cat knows that a whisker spied is not a whole mouse.

—MARGUERITE HENRY

Self-reliant like the cat—
that takes its prey to privacy,
the mouse's limp tail hanging like a shoelace
from its mouth.

—MARIANNE MOORE

So it is, and such is life. The cat's away, and the mice they
play.   —CHARLES DICKENS

The cat does not negotiate with the mouse.

—ROBERT K. MASSIE

In the time of Hoel the Good, king of Wales, who died in the year 948, laws were made as well to preserve, as to fix the different prices of animals; among which the Cat was included, as being at that period of great importance, on account of its scarcity and utility. The price of a kitten before it could see was fixed at one penny; till proof could be given of its having caught a mouse, two-pence; after which it was rated at four-pence, which was a great sum in those days.

—*A GENERAL HISTORY OF QUADRUPEDS*

A young and crafty cat in good physical and psychological condition can bring in a "bounty" of at least 1,000 mice in a year. —BILL FLEMING AND JUDY PETERSEN-FLEMING

Hunter Cat

A healthy cat, neutered at the right age and thus relieved of the demands of sex or feeding families, loves to hunt. That is the cat's job. Ecologically, the cat keeps the rodent population in balance. If you feed yours well, it will hunt for six or eight hours out of the twenty-four—*if* there is anything to hunt. —PAUL COREY

Above his nose, Mr. Forsyte has a bald patch which is often dusted with earth and sand when he comes in. Both patch and dusting are due to snuffling down rabbit-holes, a terrifying experience, surely, for the inmates; worse, I should think, than a wolf at one's door, since rabbits have no doors. —MONICA EDWARDS

For unlike a dog that will scare up a flock of birds and then rush away, a cat, even in bitter weather, will wait patiently for hours hoping to make a kill. —THALASSA CRUSO

His body melts into the ground, his eyes blazing with a primitive excitement. His tail twitches with a hypnotic effect, the body tense with each muscle rippling, storing more energy by the second. He looks like a statue coming to life. Slowly one paw creeps forward, then the next, his body compressing into a spring ready to explode. Suddenly the explosion happens ... all thirteen pounds of Fridge the tomcat pounces into the air and a young sparrow narrowly escapes.   —BILL FLEMING AND JUDY PETERSEN-FLEMING

It is remarkable, in cats, that the outer life they reveal to their master is one of perpetual confident boredom. All they betray of the hidden life is by means of symbol; if it were not for the recurring evidences of murder—the disemboweled rabbits, the headless flickers, the torn squirrels—we should forever imagine our cats to be simple pets whose highest ambition is to sleep in the best soft chair, whose worst crime is to sharpen their claws on the carpeting.

—ROBLEY WILSON, JR.

She sights a Bird—she chuckles—
She flattens—then she crawls—
She runs without the look of feet—
Her eyes increase to Balls.

—EMILY DICKINSON

Little Robin Redbreast sat upon a tree,
Up went the Pussy-cat, and down went he,
Down came Pussy-cat, away Robin ran;
Says little Robin Redbreast: 'Catch me if you
    can!'

Little Robin Redbreast jumped upon a spade,
Pussy-cat jumped after him, and then he was
    afraid.
Little Robin chirped and sang, and what did
    Pussy say?
Pussy-cat said: "Mew, mew, mew," and Robin ran
    away.

—Mother Goose

She could never be made to comprehend the great difference between fur and feathers, nor see why her mistress should gravely reprove her when she brought in a bird, and warmly commend when she brought in a mouse.

—Harriet Beecher Stowe

A lame cat is better than a swift horse when rats infest the palace.

—Proverb

This beast is wonderful nimble, setting upon her prey like a lion, by leaping.

—EDWARD TOPSELL

We have always owned cats; I grew up with them, and the house would not seem properly equipped without one. But owning a cat and keeping birds supplied with winter food tends to lead to what medical leaflets term contraindications, and in spite of our best efforts, there were in the past occasional tragedies. —THALASSA CRUSO

Did St. Francis really preach to the birds? Whatever for? If he really liked birds he would have done better to preach to the cats. —REBECCA WEST

Cats do not like prudent rats.

—H. L. Mencken

À bon chat bon rat.
A good cat deserves a good rat.

—French proverb

The Nature of Cats

Cat: A pygmy lion who loves mice, hates dogs, and patronizes human beings. —OLIVER HERFORD

Cats are not people. It's important to stress that, because excessive cat watching often leads to the delusion that cats *are* people. —DAN GREENBURG

Such is one of those big-whiskered and well-furred tomcats, that you see quiet in a corner, digesting at his leisure, sleeping if it seems good to him, sometimes giving himself the pleasure of hunting, for the rest enjoying life peaceably, without being troubled by useless reflections, and little caring to communicate his thoughts to others. Truly it needs only that a female cat come on the scene to derange all his philosophy; but are our philosophers wiser on such occasions? —FATHER BOUGEANT

Cats are like Baptists. They raise hell but you can't catch them at it. —Anonymous

Let the female cat run; the tomcat will catch her.
—German proverb

Cats are passionate and voluptuous . . .
—Sylvia Townsend Warner

One spring, when my son was little, we got a cat named Mrs. Gray who we decided to allow to have babies so that he could observe at first hand the wonder of life. She was married, obviously, so it was all right. One day she went into heat, put on her lipstick, and lay on her back out on the front lawn, rolling and moaning and smoking cigarettes by the carton, and the gentlemen cats of the neighborhood stood around and watched. They had had operations in their youth, and didn't know what was wrong. They stood around in their yards and discussed mutual funds as she moaned and sang to them, and finally a ringer came by and said, "Hi, doll," and they screamed at each other all afternoon, made love, and she raked him with her claws and drove him away. —Garrison Keillor

*O*ne cat just leads to another.

— ERNEST HEMINGWAY

A man has to work so hard so that something of his personality stays alive. A tomcat has it so easy, he has only to spray and his presence is there for years on rainy days.

— ALBERT EINSTEIN

A cat may go to a monastery, but she still remains a cat!

— AFRICAN PROVERB

Among human beings a cat is merely a cat; among cats a cat is a prowling shadow in a jungle.   —KAREL CAPEK

Curiosity killed the cat.
But satisfaction brought it back.

—PROVERB

Cats can't help being curious; it's in their genes. I realize that. But if curiosity killed the cat, this one is asking for it. Other cats are curious—this cat is downright nosy. What's inside the sink cupboards? Behind the refrigerator? Down the hot-air registers? On top of the television? Beneath the papers on my desk.   —MAYNARD GOOD STODDARD

"I suppose she will run away from me some day," Wilbur says, running his hand over Lillian's back until her fur crackles. "Yes, although I will give her plenty of liver and catnip, and one thing and another, and all my affection, she will probably give me the go-by. Cats are like women, and women are like cats. They are both very ungrateful."

—DAMON RUNYON

A cat determined not to be
found can fold itself up like
a pocket handkerchief if it
wants to.

—Dr. Louis J. Camuti

There wanst was two cats at Kilkenny,
Each thought there was one cat too many,
So they quarrell'd and fit,
They scratch'd and they bit,
Till, excepting their nails,
And the tips of their tails,
Instead of two cats, there warn't any.

—Anonymous

Cats are possessed of a shy, retiring nature, cajoling, haughty, and capricious, difficult to fathom. They reveal themselves only to certain favored individuals, and are repelled by the faintest suggestion of insult or even by the most trifling deception. —Pierre Loti

Cats do not declare their love much; they enact it, by their myriad invocations of our pleasure. —VICKI HEARNE

Cats do not go for a walk to get somewhere but to explore. —SIDNEY DENHAM

Passion for place—there is no greater urge in feline nature. —PAUL ANNIXTER

Cats don't belong to people. They belong to places.

—WRIGHT MORRIS

Cats know not how to pardon. —JEAN DE LA FONTAINE

Cats seem to go on the principle that it never does any harm to ask for what you want. —JOSEPH WOOD KRUTCH

Cats, by means of their whiskers, seem to possess something like an additional sense: these have, perhaps, some analogy to the antennae of moths and butterflies.

—REV. W. BINGLEY

Cats, like men, are flatterers.

—WILLIAM S. LANDOR

Catus amat pisces, sed non vult tangere plantas.
The cat would eat fish, and would not wet her feet.

—PROVERB

For he has the subtlety and hissing of a serpent, which in goodness he suppresses.   —CHRISTOPHER SMART

Honest as a cat when the meat is out of reach.

—ENGLISH SAYING

I don't know what the cat can have eaten. Usually I know exactly what the cat has eaten. Not only have I fed it to the cat, at the cat's keen insistence, but the cat has thrown it up on the rug and someone has tracked it all the way over onto the other rug. I don't know why cats are such habitual vomiters. They don't seem to enjoy it, judging by the sounds they make while doing it. It's in their nature. A dog is going to bark. A cat is going to vomit.   —ROY BLOUNT, JR.

In the middle of a world
that has always been a bit mad,
the cat walks with confidence.
                    —ROSEANNE AMBERSON

Most cats do not approach humans recklessly. The possibility of concealed weapons, clods or sticks, tends to make them reserved. Homeless cats in particular—with some justification, unfortunately—consider humans their natural enemies. Much ceremony must be observed, and a number of diplomatic feelers put out, before establishing a state of truce.   —LLOYD ALEXANDER

Rarely do you see a cat discomfited. They have no conscience, and they never regret.   —BARBARA WEBSTER

Cats refuse to take the blame for anything—including their own sins.   —ELIZABETH PETERS

No man has ever dared to manifest his boredom so insolently as does a Siamese tomcat.

—ALDOUS HUXLEY

So, every now and then, he went on a rove and ramble all by himself, and stayed away for hours, climbing a tree or two, or exploring a back yard several streets away, or paying a brief call at one or other of the grocers in the neighborhood, just in case a small piece of raw liver might be about. Besides he had to keep a census of the local cats, and to know what was going on, even though he chose to have no part in the ludicrous wars for position and power which ungentle, terrible cats kept up for appearance's sake. Then for a few hours at a time he forgot about his obligations and responsibilities at home and became a catly cat again. It was a great relief to dash up a tree and down again, with no one at all to watch or applaud. It was a great relief to be a cat and nothing but a cat, and to be busy with his own affairs.

—MAY SARTON

The cat does not offer services. The cat offers itself. Of course he wants care and shelter. You don't buy love for nothing. Like all pure creatures, cats are practical.

—William S. Burroughs

The cat, like the genius, draws into itself as into a shell except in the atmosphere of congeniality, and this is the secret of its remarkable and elusive personality.

—Ida M. Mellen

The more you rub a cat on the rump, the higher she sets her tail.　　　　　　—John Ray

Walking ... is a distasteful form of exercise to a cat unless he has a purpose in view.　　　　—Carl Van Vechten

Why, then, if not to steal food, would a cat go up on the counter? Why did George Mallory try to go up on Mount Everest, which was quite a lot more trouble? Because it is there. Because of the view from the kitchen window. To lick the drips from the tap in the sink. To try to open the cupboards and see what's inside them, maybe to squeeze among the glassware. Or, on a rainy day, to look for small objects to knock off onto the floor and see if they will roll.

—BARBARA HOLLAND

Most cats, when they are Out want to be In, and vice versa, and often simultaneously. —DR. LOUIS J. CAMUTI

A cat is always on the wrong side of the door.

—ANONYMOUS

Cats are like greatness: Some people are born into cat-loving families, some achieve cats, and some have cats thrust upon them. —WILLIAM H. A. CARR

Cats are only human, they have their faults.

—KINGSLEY AMIS

In many respects, cats are more like men and women than dogs; they have moods, and their nature is complex.

—HELEN WINSLOW

He lies there, purring and dreaming, shifting his limbs now and then in an ecstasy of cushioned comfort. He seems the incarnation of everything soft and silky and velvety, without a sharp edge in his composition, a dreamer whose philosophy is sleep and let sleep; and then, as evening draws on, he goes out into the garden with a red glint in his eyes and slays a drowsy sparrow.   —Saki

Cleanliness

A cat is the only domestic animal I know who toilet trains itself and does a damned impressive job of it.

—JOSEPH EPSTEIN

A cat licking herself solves most of the problems of infection. We wash too much and finally it kills us.

—WILLIAM CARLOS WILLIAMS

Cats, flies and women are ever at their toilets.

—FRENCH PROVERB

It is a neat and cleanly creature, often licking itself to keep it fair and clean, and washing its face with its fore feet.

—WILLIAM SALMON

Cleanliness in the cat world is usually a virtue put above godliness.

—CARL VAN VECHTEN

To bathe a cat takes brute force, perseverance, courage of conviction—and a cat. The last ingredient is usually hardest to come by.

           —Stephen Baker

From one cat to another:

If you have committed any kind of an error and anyone scolds you—wash. If you slip and fall off something and somebody laughs at you—wash. If somebody calls you and you don't care to come and still you don't wish to make it a direct insult—wash. Something hurt you? Wash it.

          —Paul Gallico

The Independence of Cats

It may have been noticed that I use the word "guardianship," in preference to "ownership," of a cat. "Ownership" implies authority over body and soul. A dog, in its devotion, will of its own free will accept this authority; a cat, never. This independence is offensive to people who do not care for cats: I have never been able to understand why. I can no more see why one should assume possession over an animal than over a human being. —MARGUERITE STEEN

Of all God's creatures there is only one that cannot be made the slave of the lash. That one is the cat.

—MARK TWAIN

The vanity of man revolts from the serene indifference of the cat. —AGNES REPPLIER

Alexander the Great, Napoleon, and Hitler ... were apparently terrified of small felines.... If you want to conquer the world you had better not share even a moment with an animal that refuses to be conquered at any price, by anyone.   —DESMOND MORRIS

Don't use cats—they'll screw up your data.
                              —SCIENCE PROFESSOR TO STUDENT

As soon as they're out of your sight, you are out of their mind.   —WALTER DE LA MARE

People with insufficient personalities are fond of cats. These people adore being ignored.   —HENRY MORGAN

Cats are absolute individuals, with their own ideas about everything, including the people they own.
                              —JOHN DINGMAN

Are cats lazy? Well, more power to them if they are. Which one of us has not entertained the dream of doing just as he likes, and as much as he likes? —FERNAND MÉRY

Cats have always been avoided by serious students of animal behavior. Not that cats cannot be taught to behave but because they usually behave only in the way they *feel* like behaving—which rarely coincides with anything except their immediate desires. At least, that is the assumption of the uninitiated. —KEN VON DER PORTEN

He lives in the half-lights in secret places, free and alone— this mysterious little-great being whom his mistress calls "My cat." —MARGARET BENSON

He would lie or sit with his whiskers to the North before noonday, and due South afterwards. In general his manners were perfection. But occasionally when she called him, his face would appear to knot itself into a frown—at any rate to assume a low sullen look, as if he expostulated "Why must you be interrupting me, Madam, when I am thinking of something else?" —WALTER DE LA MARE

I gave an order to a cat, and the cat gave it to its tail.

—Chinese proverb

A man without a master is a rare thing indeed; for how many of us, having one way or another escaped the bonds of filial duty, and not yet having entered into wedlock, still manage to escape the slavery of needful employment. Yet to be a cat without a master is always and forever no more than being a cat. —Robert B. Robbins

I love in the cat the independent and almost ungrateful temper which prevents it from attaching itself to anyone; the indifference with which it passes from the salon to the housetop. —François René, Vicomte de Chateaubriand

If a cat can detect no self-advantage in what it is being told to do, it says the hell with it, and, if pressure is brought to bear, it will grow increasingly surly and irritable to the point where it is hopeless to continue.

—John D. MacDonald

Insofar as it is the only one of man's domestic animals that can boast truly solitary roots, the cat is indeed an enigma, but almost certainly for the same reason, it is a very successful enigma. While it is able to form warm and lasting relationships with humans and members of its own kind (and with other animals also), it has no overwhelming need for company, and reserves the right to choose the degree of its involvement with others according to its mood or situation. For every house cat that is willing to share its home with others, one could probably find one who will absolutely refuse to do so. —JEREMY ANGEL

No tame animal has lost less of its dignity or maintained more of its ancient reserve. The domestic cat might rebel tomorrow. —WILLIAM CONWAY

One of the things most beguiling, to cat-lovers, is the intractability of a cat, its blank refusal of coercion, its refusal to surrender the least part of its spiritual independence even to those for whom it has learned to care. No one who does not understand this and accept this is fit to have the guardianship of a cat. —MARGUERITE STEEN

*She walks her chosen path by our side;
but our ways are not her ways, our
influence does not remotely reach her.*

—AGNES REPPLIER

The cat is the only animal which accepts the comforts but
rejects the bondage of domesticity.

—GEORGES, COMTE DE BUFFON

The cat is the only animal without visible means of support
who still manages to find a living in the city.

—CARL VAN VECHTEN

The most domesticated of cats somehow contrives to lead
an outside life of its own.   —KATHARINE BRIGGS

The only mystery about the cat is why it ever decided to
become a domestic animal.   —COMPTON MACKENZIE

There is no evidence that at any time during its history the
cat's way of life and its reception into human homesteads
were purposely planned and directed by humans, as was

the case with all other domestic animals, at least from a very early stage of their association.... In other words, there was no agent domesticating the cat besides the cat himself. —PAUL LEYHAUSEN

*T*o escort a cat on a leash is against the nature of the cat.

—ADLAI STEVENSON

Work—other people's work—is an intolerable idea to a cat. Can you picture cats herding sheep or agreeing to pull a cart? They will not inconvenience themselves to the slightest degree. —DR. LOUIS J. CAMUTI

It is useless to punish a cat. They have no conception of human discipline; if they do, the idea is unattractive to them.

—LLOYD ALEXANDER

The great charm of cats is their rampant egotism, their devil-may-care attitude toward responsibility, their disinclination to earn an honest dollar. —ROBERTSON DAVIES

It is a difficult matter to gain the affection of a cat. He is a philosophical animal, tenacious of his own habits, fond of order and neatness, and disinclined to extravagant sentiment. He will be your friend, if he finds you worthy of friendship, but not your slave.   —THÉOPHILE GAUTIER

A cat is there when you call her—if she doesn't have something better to do.

—BILL ADLER

The really great thing about cats is their endless variety. One can pick a cat to fit almost any kind of decor, color scheme, income, personality, mood. But under the fur, whatever color it may be, there still lies, essentially unchanged, one of the world's free souls.   —ERIC GURNEY

A human may go for a stroll with a cat; he has to walk a dog. The cat leads the way, running ahead, tail high, making sure you understand the arrangement. If you should happen to get ahead, the cat will never allow you to think it is following you. It will stop and clean some hard-to-reach spot, or investigate a suspicious movement in the grass; you will find yourself waiting and fidgeting like the lackey you are. But this is not annoying to cat lovers, who understand and appreciate a good joke, even when it is on them.

—ROBERT STEARNS

"What is the appeal about cats?" he said kindly. "I've always wanted to know."

"They don't care if you like them. They haven't the slightest notion of gratitude, and they never pretend. They take what you have to offer, and away they go."

—MAVIS GALLANT

Is it yet another survival of jungle instinct, this hiding away from prying eyes at important times? Or merely a gesture of independence, a challenge to man and his stupid ways?

—MICHAEL JOSEPH

The cat lives alone, has no need of society, obeys only when she pleases, pretends to sleep that she may see the more clearly, and scratches everything on which she can lay her paw.   —FRANÇOIS RENÉ, VICOMTE DE CHATEAUBRIAND

It is in the nature of cats to do a certain amount of unescorted roaming.

—ADLAI STEVENSON

Smart Cats

Anyone who has ever known a cat really well feels that this cat is superior to most Harvard professors in brain power.
—GLADYS TABOR

Cats ... can read your character better than a $50 an hour psychiatrist.
—PAUL GALLICO

Cats always know whether people like or dislike them. They do not always care enough to do anything about it.
—WINIFRED CARRIERE

Cats know how to obtain food without labor, shelter without confinement, and love without penalties.   —W. L. GEORGE

A cat is nobody's fool.
—HEYWOOD BROUN

Cats love one so much—more than they will allow.
But they have so much wisdom they keep it to
themselves.

—MARY WILKINS

Cats virtually always underestimate human intelligence
just as we, perhaps, underestimate theirs.

—ROGER A. CARAS

Even overweight cats instinctively know the cardinal rule:
when fat, arrange yourself in slim poses.   —JOHN WEITZ

*Everything that moves serves to interest
and amuse a cat.*

—AUGUSTIN-PARADIS DE MONCRIF

I have studied many philosophers and many cats. The wisdom of cats is infinitely superior.   —HIPPOLYTE TAINE

If a cat does something, we call it instinct; if we do the same thing, for the same reason, we call it intelligence.

—WILL CUPPY

Intelligence in the cat is underrated. —LOUIS WAIN

Most people don't know that cats understand people talk. We are born with that knowledge. It doesn't matter whether it's Micronesian or Asiatic or English or Whatever, we understand it. A cat can't make words. Our voice box is different from the human kind. But we understand spoken words.

—DOROTHY B. HUGHES

It's funny how dogs and cats know the inside of folks better than other folks do, isn't it?

—ELEANOR H. PORTER

Long contact with the human race has developed in it [the cat] the art of diplomacy, and no Roman Catholic in medieval days knew better how to ingratiate himself with his surroundings than a cat with a saucer of cream on its horizon.

—SAKI

The cat seldom interferes with other people's rights. His intelligence keeps him from doing many of the fool things that complicate life. —CARL VAN VECHTEN

The smart cat doesn't let on that he is.

—H. G. FROMMER

Before him, cats were depicted as either stupid or sinister. But cats are smart. Heathcliff represents the anti-hero, like Humphrey Bogart. He's a tough little mug.

—GEORGE GATELY

Quite obviously a cat trusts human beings; but she doesn't trust another cat because she knows better than we do.

—KAREL CAPEK

Watch a cat when it enters a room for the first time. It searches and smells about, it is not quiet for a moment, it trusts nothing until it has examined and made acquaintance with everything. —JEAN JACQUES ROUSSEAU

*Some Cats is blind,
and stone-deaf some,
But ain't no Cat
wuz ever dumb.*

—ANTHONY HENDERSON EUWER

Cats and Water

It is the popular belief that cats have an inherent dislike for water, and in general they are catabaptists, but my Ariel had no aversion to water; indeed, this orange Persian puss was accustomed to leap voluntarily into my warm morning tub, and she particularly liked to sit in the wash-hand bowl under the open faucet. —CARL VAN VECHTEN

One day when I was paying an urgent visit to the loo ... I was absolutely rushing, but he beat me to it by about two seconds, and shot under me as I was about to sit down, and, of course, almost got a concussion, because he went crashing to the bottom of the basin of the loo and raised a big lump on his head. He was extremely heavy to lift out, because he'd swallowed a great deal of water. —BERYL REID

The cat Bastet sat perched on the rim of the tub, watching me through slitted golden eyes. She was fascinated by baths. I suppose total immersion in water must have seemed to her a peculiar method of cleansing oneself.

—ELIZABETH PETERS

A cat is much delighted to play with her image in a glass, and if at any time she behold it in water, presently she leapeth down into the water which naturally she doth abhor. Nothing is more contrary to the nature of a cat than is wet and water and for this cause came the proverb that they love not to wet their feet.   —EDWARD TOPSELL

Now, as you all know, there is nothing a cat dislikes so much as water; just watch your kitty shake her paws daintily when she steps into a puddle, and see how disgusted she is if a drop of water falls on her nose and back.

—AGNES A. SANDHAM

Why people should prefer a wet cat to a dry one I have never been able to understand; but that a wet cat is practically sure of being taken in and gushed over, while a dry cat is liable to have the garden hose turned upon it, is an undoubted fact.   —JEROME K. JEROME

Cats at Night

The cat has always been associated with the moon. Like the moon it comes to life at night, escaping from humanity and wandering over housetops with its eyes beaming out through the darkness. —PATRICIA DALE-GREEN

De noche todos los Gatos son pardos.
By night all cats are grey.

—CERVANTES

One of the Clock, and silence deep
Then up the Stairway, black and steep
The old House-Cat comes creepy-creep
With soft feet goes from room to room
Her green eyes shining through the gloom,
And finds all fast asleep.

—KATHARINE PYLE

The Egyptians have observed
in the eyes of a cat,
the increase of the moonlight.

—EDWARD TOPSELL

The cat that comes to my window sill
When the moon looks cold and the night is
    still—
He comes in a frenzied state alone
With a tail that stands like a pine tree cone,
And says: "I have finished my evening lark,
And I think I can hear a hound dog bark.
My whiskers are froze and stuck to my chin.
I do wish you'd git up and let me in."
That cat gits in.

—BEN KING

The cat went here and there
And the moon spun round like a top,
And the nearest kin of the moon,
The creeping cat, looked up.

Black Minnaloushe stared at the moon,
For, wander and wail as he would,
The pure cold light in the sky
Troubled his animal blood.
Minnaloushe runs in the grass
Lifting his delicate feet.
Do you dance, Minnaloushe, do you dance?
                    —WILLIAM BUTLER YEATS

Within that porch, across the way,
I see two naked eyes this night;
Two eyes that neither shut nor blink,
Searching my face with a green light.

But cats to me are strange, so strange
I cannot sleep if one is near;
And though I'm sure I see those eyes,
I'm not so sure a body's there!
                    —WILLIAM HENRY DAVIES

*The cat laps moonbeams in the bowl of
water, thinking them to be milk.*
                    —HINDU PROVERB

Wild Cats

The cat keeps his side of the bargain.... He will kill mice, and he will be kind to babies when he is in the house, just so long as they do not pull his tail too hard. But when he has done that, and between times, and when the moon gets up and night comes, he is the Cat that walks by himself, and all places are alike to him. Then he goes out to the Wet Wild Woods or up on the Wet Wild Trees or on the Wet Wild Roofs, waving his wild tail and walking by his wild lone.

—RUDYARD KIPLING

For he counteracts the Devil, who is death, by
    brisking about the life.
For in his morning orisons he loves the sun and
    the sun loves him.
For he is of the tribe of Tiger.

—CHRISTOPHER SMART

A cat is a tiger that is fed by hand.   —YAKAOKA GENRIN

God made the cat in order that man might have the pleasure of caressing the tiger.

—Fernand Méry

His extraordinary size, his daring, and his utter lack of sympathy soon made him the leader—and, at the same time, the terror—of all the loose-lived cats in a wide neighborhood. He contracted no friendships and had no confidants. He seldom slept in the same place twice in succession, and though he was wanted by the police, he was not found. In appearance he did not lack distinction of an ominous sort; the slow, rhythmic, perfectly controlled mechanism of his tail, as he impressively walked abroad, was incomparably sinister. This stately and dangerous walk of his, his long, vibrant whiskers, his scars, his yellow eye, so ice cold, so fire-hot, haughty as the eye of Satan, gave him the deadly air of a mousequetaire duelist. His soul was in that walk and in that eye; it could be read—the soul of a bravo of fortune, living on his wits and his valour, asking no favours and granting no quarter. Intolerant, proud, sullen, yet watchful and constantly planning—purely a militarist, believing in slaughter as in religion, and confident that art, science, poetry, and the good of the world were happily advanced thereby—Gipsy had become, though technically not a wild cat, undoubtedly the most untamed cat at large in the civilized world.　　　　　　　　—BOOTH TARKINGTON

When she walked ... she stretched out long and thin like a little tiger, and held her head high to look over the grass as if she were threading the jungle.　—SARAH ORNE JEWETT

A cat pent up becomes a lion.
　　　　　—ITALIAN PROVERB

At whiles it seems as if one were somewhat as the cats, which ever have appeared to me to be animals of two parts, the one of the house and the cushion and the prepared food, the other that is free of the night and runs wild with the wind in its coat and the smell of the earth in its nostrils.
　　　　　　　　　　—UNA L. SILBERRAD

Give her but a wavering leaf-shadow of a breeze combing the grasses and she was back a million years, glaring with night-lit eyes in the thickets, projecting a terrible aura of fear that stilled and quelled all creatures.

—Paul Annixter

Lately a small tabby cat has come every day and stared at me with a strange, intense look. Of course I put food out, night and morning. She is so terrified that she runs away at once when I open the door, but she comes back to eat ravenously as soon as I disappear. Yet her hunger is clearly not only for food. I long to take her in my arms and hear her purr with relief at finding shelter. Will she ever become tame enough for that, to give in to what she longs to have? It is such an intense look with which she scans my face at the door before she runs away. It is not a pleading look, simply a huge question: "Can I trust?" Our two gazes hang on its taut thread. I find it painful.   —May Sarton

My cat is a lion in a jungle of small bushes.

—English proverb

Of all the domesticated animals in the world, the cat has been domesticated the shortest duration of time.

—Bill Fleming and Judy Petersen-Fleming

*P*rowling his own quiet backyard or asleep by the fire, he is still only a whisker away from the wilds.

—JEAN BURDEN

Since our housecat no longer has to hunt, she may spend hours dreaming and philosophizing. Perhaps when she sleeps, she dreams of the wild.

—JOHN RICHARD STEPHENS

That which in the wild cat is but the stealthy cunning of the hunter is refined in the tame one into a habitual gentleness.   —PHILIP GILBERT HAMERTON

The cat is domestic only as far as it suits its own ends.

—SAKI

The cat is not really a domestic animal, and his chief charm lies in the fact that he still walks by himself.

—KONRAD LORENZ

> The greater cats with golden eyes
> Stare out between the bars.
> Deserts are there, and different skies,
> And night with different stars.
>
> —VITA SACKVILLE-WEST

The wildcat is the "real" cat, the soul of the domestic cat; unknowable to human beings, he yet exists inside our household pets, who have long ago seduced us with their seemingly civilized ways.   —JOYCE CAROL OATES

This switch from tame pet to wild animal and then back again is fascinating to watch. Any cat owner who has accidentally come across the pet cat when it is deeply involved in some feline soap opera of sex and violence will know what I mean. One instant the animal is totally wrapped up in an intense drama of courtship and status. Then out of the corner of its eye it spots its human owner watching the proceedings. There is a schizoid moment of double involvement, a hesitation, and the animal runs across, rubs against its owner's leg, and becomes the house kitten once more.

—DESMOND MORRIS

We tie bright ribbons around their necks, and occasionally little tinkling bells, and we affect to think that they are as sweet and vapid as the coy name "kitty" by which we call them would imply. It is a curious illusion. For purring beside our fireplaces and pattering along our back fences, we have got a wild beast as uncowed and uncorrupted as any under heaven.   —ALAN DEVOE

The cat of the slums and alleys, starved, outcast, harried, still keeps amid the prowlings of its adversity the bold, free, panther-tread with which it paced of yore the temple courts of Thebes, still displays the self-reliant watchfulness which man has never taught it to lay aside.   —SAKI

There is some truth to the assertion that the cat, with the exception of a few luxury breeds ... is no domestic animal but a completely wild being.   —KONRAD LORENZ

The phrase "domestic cat" is an oxymoron.

—GEORGE F. WILL

Kittens

Once upon a time there were three little kittens, and their names were Mittens, Tom Kitten, and Moppet.

They had dear little fur coats of their own; and they tumbled about the doorstep and played in the dust.

—BEATRIX POTTER

Kittens, kittens, showers of kittens, visitations of kittens. So many, you see them as Kitten, like leaves growing on a bare branch, staying heavy and green, then falling exactly the same every year. People coming to visit say: What happened to that lovely kitten? What lovely kitten? They are all lovely kittens.

—DORIS LESSING

No matter how much cats fight, there always seem to be plenty of kittens.

—ABRAHAM LINCOLN

While Alice was sitting curled up in a corner of the great armchair, half talking to herself and half asleep, the kitten had been having a grand game of romps with the ball of worsted Alice had been trying to wind up, and had been rolling it up and down till it had all come undone again; and there it was, spread over the hearth-rug, all knots and tangles, with the kitten running after its own tail in the middle.   —LEWIS CARROLL

A cat with kittens nearly always decides sooner or later to move them.   —SIDNEY DENHAM

A kitten is so flexible that she is almost double; the hind parts are equivalent to another kitten with which the fore-part plays. She does not discover that her tail belongs to her until you tread on it.   —HENRY DAVID THOREAU

A kitten is the most irresistible comedian in the world. Its wide-open eyes gleam with wonder and mirth, it darts madly at nothing at all, and then, as though suddenly checked in the pursuit, prances sideways on its hind legs with ridiculous agility and zeal.   —AGNES REPPLIER

A kitten is the delight of a household.
All day long a comedy is played by this
incomparable actor.

—JULES CHAMPFLEURY

An ordinary kitten will ask more questions than any five-year-old boy.   —CARL VAN VECHTEN

As a kitten, this cat never slept on the outside of the bed. She waited until I was in it, then she walked all over me, considering the possibilities.   —DORIS LESSING

Ez soshubble ez a baskit er kittens.

—JOEL CHANDLER HARRIS

But buds will be roses,
and kittens, cats,
—more's the pity.

        —LOUISA MAY ALCOTT

But you must not think we allowed our kittens to behave badly. On the contrary, we tried all we could to teach them good manners. But even so, they tore up an old pair of

Dora's shoes, they scratched the polished furniture, and clawed the new leather for the delight of exercising their pin-like nails. —ERNEST NISTER

Confront a child, a puppy, and a kitten with sudden danger; the child will turn instinctively for assistance, the puppy will grovel in abject submission to the impending visitation, the kitten will brace its tiny body for a frantic resistance.

—SAKI

Even people who dislike cats find it difficult to dislike kittens. Cardinal Richelieu (1585–1642), the French statesman, liked kittens so much that he kept dozens of them for his amusement. Preferring them to cats, he replaced the kittens with more kittens as they grew older.

—JOHN RICHARD STEPHENS

Cats mean kittens, plentiful and frequent. —DORIS LESSING

Four little Persians, but one only looked in my direction. I extended a tentative finger and two soft paws clung to it. There was a contented sound of purring, I suspect on both our parts.   —GEORGE FREEDLEY

> Gather kittens while you may,
> Time brings only sorrow;
> And the kittens of today
> Will be old cats tomorrow.
>   —OLIVER HERFORD

He is in youth swift, pliant and merry, and leapeth and rusheth on all thing that is before him; and is lead by a straw and playeth therewith. —BARTHOLOMAEUS ANGLICUS

His markings, month by month, became more beautiful, lines of autumn bracken colours with shapes which reminded me of currents on a quiet sea. True that at times his head, because of his youth, looked scraggy, even his body sometimes looked scraggy, but suddenly for some reason like the change of light, or of mood, he looked his potential. This was going to be a champion cat.

—DEREK TANGYE

I have just been given a very engaging Persian kitten, named after St. Philip Neri (who was very sound on cats) and his opinion is that *I* have been given to *him*.

—EVELYN UNDERHILL

If "The child is father of the man," why is not the kitten father of the cat? If in the little boy there lurks the infant likeness of all that manhood will complete, why does not the kitten betray some of the attributes common to the adult puss? A puppy is but a dog, plus high spirits, and minus common sense. We never hear our friends say they love puppies, but cannot bear dogs. A kitten is a thing apart; and many people who lack the discriminating enthusiasm for cats, who regard these beautiful beasts with aversion and mistrust, are won over easily, and cajoled out of their prejudices by the deceitful wiles of kittenhood.

—AGNES REPPLIER

In Maine of course kittens are not so important as cows; but they have their place in nearly every house, sometimes as commodities, sometimes as guardians of the grain bags and chicken coops, sometimes as pets.

—ELIZABETH COATSWORTH

It is a very inconvenient habit of kittens (Alice had once made the remark) that, whatever you say to them, they always purr.
—Lewis Carroll

Kittens believe that all nature is occupied with their diversion.
—Augustin-Paradis de Moncrif

Wild beasts he created later,
Lions with their paws so furious;
In the image of the lion
Made he kittens small and curious.
—Heinrich Heine

See the Kitten on the wall,
Sporting with the leaves that fall,
Withered leaves—one, two and three—
From the lofty elder tree!

But the Kitten, how she starts,
Crouches, stretches, paws and darts!
First at one, and then its fellow
Just as light and just as yellow.
—WILLIAM WORDSWORTH

A kitten is chiefly remarkable for rushing about like mad at nothing whatever, and generally stopping before it gets there.

—AGNES REPPLIER

The kitten was awake, though, and thinking. About what? Being unfamiliar with real life, and having no store of impressions, he could think only instinctually, and envision life only according to those notions he had inherited, together with his flesh and blood, from his tiger ancestors. (*Vide* Dar-

win.) His thoughts were on the order of daydreams. His feline imagination pictures something like the Arabian desert,
across which moved shadows very much resembling
Praskovya, the stove, the broom.   —Anton Chekhov

The kittens, White and White, never leave me. Because I
recently had the kitchen floor done over in white tile, I am
always close to trampling a White; in the dark, when I
grope for my shearling slippers, my bare foot prods a
White. By day I think I am seeing things as they trot along
amiably beside me; when I stop they repose on the tops
of my feet, like rosettes of whipped cream.

    —Katinka Loeser

The playful kitten, with its pretty tigerish gambols, is infinitely more amusing than half the people one is obliged to
live with in the world.   —Lady Sidney Morgan

The three merriest things in the world are a cat's kitten, a
goat's kid, and a young widow.   —Irish proverb

The trouble with a kitten is
THAT
Eventually it becomes a
CAT.

—OGDEN NASH

There is no more intrepid explorer than a kitten.
—JULES CHAMPFLEURY

Those dear, sweet little lumps, stumping and padding about the house, pulling over electric lamps, making little puddles in slippers, crawling up my legs, on to my lap (my legs scratched by them, like Lazarus's), I see myself finding a kitten in the sleeve when I'm putting on my coat, and my tie under the bed when I want to put it on. —KAREL CAPEK

When I grow up I mean to be
A Lion large and fierce to see.
I'll mew so loud that Cook in fright
Will give me all the cream in sight.
And anyone who dares to say
"Poor Puss" to me will rue the day.
Then having swallowed him I'll creep
Into the Guest Bed Room to sleep.

—OLIVER HERFORD

We quickly discovered that two kittens were much more fun than one.
— Allen Lacy

Whatever is born of a cat will catch mice.
— Italian proverb

When kittens nap in pansy beds
And drowse the sunny hours,
I can't tell which are spotted cats
And which are spotted flowers!
— Beryl Swift

You may ... if you try hard enough, be able to enter into a very small part of a cat's world.... But the world of a kitten is almost impenetrable and you must rest content, mostly, to play the role of spectator. Unless you are tragically handicapped by the lack of any sense of humor you should be able to enjoy yourself. —PHILIP BROWN

what in hell
have i done to deserve
all these kittens
—DON MARQUIS

Now where Lillian comes from in the first place of course nobody knows. The chances are somebody chucks her out of a window into the snow, because people are always chucking kittens, and one thing and another, out of windows in New York. In fact, if there is one thing this town has plenty of, it is kittens, which finally grow up to be cats, and go snooping around ash cans, and mer-owing on roofs, and keeping people from sleeping well.
—DAMON RUNYON

*Young kittens assume that all other
animals are cats, approach them with
jaunty friendliness and invite them to
play.*

—MURIEL BEADLE

As one who has long been a pushover for cats, I should like
to offer a packet of color-fast, preshrunk advice: If a stray
kitten bounds out of nowhere when you're taking a walk,
mews piteously, and rubs a soft shoulder against your leg,
flee to the hills until the danger is over.

—MURRAY ROBINSON

Kittens can happen to anyone.   —PAUL GALLICO

Maternal Cat

I was once told a pleasant story of an English cat who had reared several large families, and who, dozing one day before the nursery fire, was disturbed and annoyed by the whining of a fretful child. She bore it as long as she could, waiting for the nurse to interpose her authority; then, finding passive endurance had outstripped the limits of her patience, she arose, crossed the room, jumped on the sofa, and twice with her strong soft paw, which had chastised many an errant kitten, deliberately boxed the little girl's ears—after which she returned to her slumbers.

—AGNES REPPLIER

Few animals exhibit more maternal tenderness, or show a greater love for their offspring, than the cat.

—REV. W. BINGLEY

In a dark, hidden crevice, safe between bales of hay, lay the gold-spattered black mother cat, Old Puss, with her five new kittens. Three were a rich yellow, one a dashing black and white, one all white.... Old Puss was glad of our visit and our offerings of roast pork and potatoes. Neither she nor we mentioned the fact that we had been earnestly hunting her hiding place for the last ten days. Now she stretched out her long legs, kneading her claws happily in the clean hay, and let us pick up her kittens and examine each one at leisure.

The gold-spattered cat was, understandably, somewhat smug. She had kept us guessing until the kittens were old enough to be handled, and she was ready to have us help take over the responsibility of their upbringing. Being extremely clever, she let us think we had finally outwitted her. —RACHEL PEDEN

Round, gray, plump-jowled like a grandmother, she washed, ate, and saw to it that she and her offspring went outside for calls of nature as regularly as any privy-bound housewife. With a recipe written in cat language, she could have baked cookies or fried a chicken. —JESSAMYN WEST

The Cat that always wears Silk Mittens
Will catch no Mice to feed her Kittens.
—ARTHUR GUITERMAN

The way Dinah washed her children's faces was this: first she held the poor thing down by its ears with one paw, and then with the other paw she rubbed its face all over, the wrong way, beginning at the nose: and just now, as I said, she was hard at work on the white kitten, which was lying quite still and trying to purr—no doubt feeling that it was all meant for the good. —LEWIS CARROLL

There is, however, one contingency in which a cat may make a prolonged and earnest attack in this hunchbacked attitude, and that is when she is defending her young. In this case she approaches her enemy when he is some distance away and she moves in a peculiar fashion, galloping with an up and down and

sideways motion, for she must continually present her imposing broadside to the foe. Though this broadside gallop with laterally held tail is seldom to be seen in real earnest, it can very often be observed in the play of young cats. I have never seen it in mature tomcats except in play, for there is no situation in which they are obliged to attack an enemy like this. In the suckling female cat, this broadside attack brings with it an absolute and unconditional readiness for self-sacrifice, and, in this state, even the gentlest cat is almost invincible. I have seen large dogs, notorious cat killers, capitulate and flee before such an attack. Ernest Thompson Seton graphically describes a charming and doubtless true occurrence in which a mother cat in Yellowstone Park put a bear to flight and pursued him until he climbed a tree in terror.

—Konrad Lorenz

Nine Lives

One of the most striking differences between a cat and a lie is that a cat has only nine lives. —MARK TWAIN

> A cat in despondency sighed,
> And resolved to commit suicide;
> She passed under the wheels
> of eight automobiles,
> And after the ninth one she died.
> —ANONYMOUS

Throw a cat over a house and it will land on its feet.
—ENGLISH PROVERB

He's like a cat; fling him which way you will, he'll light on his legs. —JOHN RAY

A cat has nine lives.
—ENGLISH PROVERB

Not Everybody Loves a Cat

"Oh, I beg your pardon," cried Alice hastily, afraid that she had hurt the poor animal's feelings, "I quite forgot you didn't like cats."

"Not like cats!" cried the mouse, in a shrill, passionate voice. "Would you like cats if you were me?"

"Well perhaps not," said Alice in a soothing tone.

—LEWIS CARROLL

A cat, I realize, cannot be everyone's cup of fur.

—JOSEPH EPSTEIN

A man who was loved by 300 women singled me out to live with him. Why? I was the only one without a cat.

—ELAYNE BOOSLER

Cat hate reflects an ugly, stupid, loutish, bigoted spirit.

—WILLIAM S. BURROUGHS

Confound the cats! All cats—always—
Cats of all colours, black, white and grey;
By night a nuisance and by day—
Confound the cats!

—ORLANDO DOBBIN

I am furious with the grey cat. The wicked creature has just robbed me of a young pigeon that I was warming by the fire. The poor little thing was beginning to revive; I had meant to tame it; it would have grown fond of me; and now all this ends in its getting crunched up by a cat. What disappointments there are in life! —ELIZABETH DRINKER

Cruel, but composed and bland,
Dumb, inscrutable and grand,
So Tiberius might have sat,
Had Tiberius been a cat.

—MATTHEW ARNOLD

I suspect that many an ailurophobe hates cats only because he feels they are better people than he is—more honest, more secure, more loved, more whatever he is not.

—WINIFRED CARRIERE

I could half persuade myself that the word felonious is derived from the feline temper.

—ROBERT SOUTHEY

Late that night Hungry Joe dreamed that Huple's cat was sleeping on his face, suffocating him, and when he woke up, Huple's cat was sleeping on his face. His agony was terrifying, the piercing unearthly howl with which he split the moonlit dark vibrating in its own impact for seconds afterward like a devastating shock. A numbing silence followed, and then a riotous din rose from inside his tent.

—JOSEPH HELLER

*B*eware *of people who dislike cats.*
                              —IRISH PROVERB

It is said that he [Alexander the Great] would swoon at the sight of a cat. Fearless before armies, indifferent to personal danger, the man who legend says wept because there were no more nations to conquer, no more armies to annihilate, was terrified of a house cat.

What is there about the cat that so threatens, or perhaps frustrates, world conquerors?   —ROGER A. CARAS

Even the tamest cats are not under the smallest subjugation, but may rather be said to enjoy perfect liberty; for they act to please themselves only; and it is impossible to retain them a moment after they choose to go off. Besides, most cats are half wild. They know not their masters, and only frequent barns, offices, or kitchens, when pressed with hunger.   —GEORGES, COMTE DE BUFFON

There are some who, if a cat accidentally come into the room, though they will neither see it nor are told of it, will presently be in a sweat and ready to die away.
                              —INCREASE MATHER

I'm one of those wretched people who can't stand cats. I don't mean just that I prefer dogs. I mean that the presence of a cat in the same room with me makes me feel like nothing on earth. I can't describe it, but I believe quite a lot of people are affected that way. Something to do with electricity, or so they tell me. I've read that very often the dislike is mutual, but it isn't so with me. The brutes seem to find me abominably fascinating, make a beeline for my legs every time. It's a funny sort of complaint, and it doesn't make me at all popular with dear old ladies.

—DOROTHY L. SAYERS

> Some men there are love not a gaping pig;
> Some, that are mad if they behold a cat.
>   —WILLIAM SHAKESPEARE

They smell and they snarl and they scratch; they have a singular aptitude for shredding rugs, drapes and upholstery; they're sneaky, selfish and not particularly smart; they are disloyal, condescending and totally useless in any rodent-free environment.

—JEAN-MICHEL CHAPEREAU

People who hate cats were rats in another incarnation.

—PROVERB

Tradition has it that Adolf Hitler hated cats. He probably did; everything else was wrong with him. Napoleon also hated cats. There are endlessly repeated stories about the French emperor and his problem. On one such occasion, it is said, he was heard calling hoarsely for help from his tent. Aides rushed in expecting to find an assassin at work and found Napoleon alone instead, sword drawn, doing battle with the rich tapestry hangings he enjoyed having around him. He insisted that he had either seen or could sense a cat lurking somewhere behind them. He was gasping for breath, red in the face, near collapse. He had to be helped to his bed, and a doctor called in to settle him down. How much of that is just more Napoleonic lore, of which there is a great deal, and how much truth is difficult to determine, but clearly the man who would conquer the world could not overcome an unreasoning dread of a small, harmless, companion animal.   —ROGER A. CARAS

Some people don't like cats. Some cats don't like people. We try to like all people. We do try. At least, some of us do.

But, after all, how can we like people who don't like us?
—Dorothy B. Hughes

Cats are oppressed; dogs terrify them, landladies starve them, boys stone them, everybody speaks of them with contempt. If they were human beings we could talk of their oppressors with a studied violence, add our strength to theirs, even organize the oppressed and like good politicians sell our charity for power. —William Butler Yeats

Work was like cats were supposed to be; if you disliked and feared it and tried to keep out of its way, it knew at once and sought you out. —Kingsley Amis

The cry of the Cat is loud, piercing, and clamorous; and whether expressive of anger or of love, is equally violent and hideous. Its call may be heard at a great distance; and is so well known to the whole fraternity, that on some occasions several hundred Cats have been brought together from different parts. Invited by the piercing cries of distress from a suffering fellow-creature, they assemble in crowds; and, with loud squalls and yells, express their horrid sympathies. —*A General History of Quadrupeds*

Cats have a curious effect on people. They seem to excite more extreme sentiments than any other animals. There are people who cannot remain in the room with a cat—who feel instinctively the presence of a cat even though they do not actually see it. On the other hand, there are people who, whatever they may be doing, will at once get up and fondle a cat immediately they see it.   —ARTHUR PONSONBY

Let us love dogs; let us love only dogs! Men and cats are unworthy creatures.   —MARIE BASHKIRTSEFF

Cats vs. Dogs

Cats are smarter than dogs. You can't get eight cats to pull a sled through snow. —JEFF VALDEZ

A cat will sit washing his face within two inches of a dog in the most frantic state of barking rage, if the dog be chained. —CARL VAN VECHTEN

A dog will often steal a bone,
But conscience lets him not alone,
And by his tail his guilt is known.

But cats consider theft a game,
And, howsoever you may blame,
Refuse the slightest sign of shame.
When food mysteriously goes,
The chances are that Pussy knows
More than she leads you to suppose.
—ANONYMOUS

Dogs come when they're called; cats take a message and get back to you.

—Missy Dizick and Mary Bly

Artists like cats; soldiers like dogs.   —Desmond Morris

To respect the cat is the beginning of the aesthetic sense. At a stage of culture when utility governs all of its judgments, mankind prefers the dog.   —Erasmus Darwin

By and large, people who enjoy teaching animals to roll over will find themselves happier with a dog.

—Barbara Holland

Cats are not dogs! ... Cats ... are selfish. A man waits on a cat hand and foot for weeks, humouring its lightest whim, and then it goes and leaves him flat because it has found a place down the road where the fish is more frequent.

—P. G. Wodehouse

Cats are dainty patricians, whereas dogs, whatever their social status, retain a *parvenu's* lack of cleanliness, and are irredeemably vulgar.   —Pierre Loti

Cats are the ultimate narcissists. You can tell this because of all the time they spend on personal grooming. Dogs aren't like this. A dog's idea of personal grooming is to roll in dead fish.   —James Gorman

Cats are to dogs what modern people are to the people we used to have. Cats are slimmer, cleaner, more attractive, disloyal, and lazy. It's easy to understand why the cat has eclipsed the dog as modern America's favorite pet. People like pets to possess the same qualities they do. Cats are irresponsible and recognize no authority, yet are completely dependent on others for their material needs. Cats cannot be made to do anything useful. Cats are mean for the fun of it. In fact, cats possess so many of the same qualities as some people (expensive girlfriends, for instance) that it's often hard to tell the people and the cats apart.

                                        —P. J. O'Rourke

*D*ogs *instinctively realize that cats are smarter than they are, so they resent the intrusion of a cat upon the household.*

—Eric Gurney

Dogs remember faces, cats places. —English saying

Dogs, then, had been entities in my life. Cats, as if they were wasps with four legs, had been there to shoo away. They did not belong in my life nor in my family's life. All of us were united that whenever we saw a cat the most important thing to do was to see it out of sight.

—Derek Tangye

*E*ven *the stupidest cat seems to know more than any dog.*

—Eleanor Clark

Finally, as regards the canine tribe, it cannot be denied that there are good dogs, very good dogs; dogs that look up at you with the most lovable eyes. Personally, I must confess that I have felt considerable esteem and affection for some of them. All the same, I share the opinion of the Orientals, who rather despise the dog as being tainted with filthy instincts, whilst they respect and fear the cat as a sort of little sphinx.   —Pierre Loti

I feared cats. Dogs were wonderfully comforting because they *wanted* to love and be loved. Cats were aloof things. They judged humanity in a cool, remote fashion which was unnerving to anyone who was a dog lover. A dog increases a man's confidence, a cat can dim it; and I have known dog lovers to be so unnerved by the presence of a cat that they have set a trap for it; and then removed it from the neighborhood.   —Derek Tangye

I shall show how wrong it is to think that the cat, the proudest and most upright of our domestic animals, is "deceitful." At the same time, I do not regard this inability to deceive as a sign of the cat's superiority. In fact, I regard it as a sign of the much higher intelligence of the dog that it is able to do so.   —Konrad Lorenz

If a dog jumps up into your lap, it is because he is fond of you; but if a cat does the same thing, it is because your lap is warmer.
——ALFRED NORTH WHITEHEAD

If animals could speak, the dog would be a blundering, outspoken, honest fellow—but the cat would have the rare grace of never saying a word too much.
——PHILIP GILBERT HAMERTON

Man loves the dog because the dog is fool enough to trust Man. On the other hand, the cat obeys the Scriptures: "Put not thy trust in things." The cat is like the wise man: he trusts a principle; not a man of principle.

—MELVIN B. TOLSON

Robert Graves once said that he wrote novels for the money he needed to live so he could write poetry. His books of prose, he said, were the show dogs he raised to support his cat. I guess a cat is sort of like a poem. A cat is relatively short. A cat is only subtly demonstrative. To be sure, you can curl up with a good cat, but that doesn't mean you *understand* the cat. A dog is like Dickens.

—ROY BLOUNT, JR.

*T*he Dog gives himself the Airs of a Cat.

—SIR RICHARD STEELE

The cat is a creature of the most refined and subtle perceptions naturally. The contrast in this respect between cats and other animals is very striking. I will not wrong the noble canine nature so far as to say that it has no delicacy, but its delicacy is not of this kind, not in actual touch, as the cat's is. The motions of the cat, being always governed by the most refined sense of touch in the animal world, are typical in quite a perfect way of what we call tact in the human world. And as a man who has tact exercises it on all occasions for his own satisfaction, even when there is no positive need for it, so a cat will walk daintily and observantly everywhere, whether amongst the glasses on a dinner table or the rubbish in a farmyard.

—ROGER A. CARAS

The cat, an aristocrat, merits our esteem, while the dog is only a scurvy type who got his position by low flatteries.

—ALEXANDRE DUMAS

The dog may be man's best friend, but it is rarely allowed out on its own to wander from garden to garden or street to street. The obedient dog has to be taken for a walk. The headstrong cat walks alone. —DESMOND MORRIS

Why, I wonder, should a great many good men and women cherish an unreasonable grudge against one animal because it does not chance to possess the precise qualities of another? "My dog fetches my slippers for me every night," said a friend triumphantly, not long ago. "He puts them first to warm by the fire, and then brings them over to my chair, wagging his tail, and as proud as Punch. Would your cat do as much for you, I'd like to know?" Assuredly not! If I waited for Agrippina to fetch my shoes or slippers, I should have no other recourse but to join as speedily as possible one of the barefooted religious orders of Italy.

—Agnes Repplier

To Someone Very Good and Just,
Who has proved worthy of her trust,
A Cat will sometimes condescend—
The Dog is Everybody's Friend.
                              —Oliver Herford

Anybody, but *anybody*, any lout, any half-wit, any scruffy, self-centered moron, can command the affection and the servile obedience of a dog, but it takes intelligence and understanding—sometimes I think a certain psychic rapport—to win the affection of a cat.

—Beverley Nichols

*Again I must remind you that
A Dog's a Dog—A Cat's a Cat.*

—T. S. Eliot

When I was young, I wanted a dog and we had no money ... I couldn't get a dog because it was too much and they finally opened up in my neighborhood in Flatbush, a damaged-pet shop. They sold damaged pets at discount, you know, you could get a bent pussy cat if you wanted; a straight camel, you know. I got a dog that stuttered. Like, cats would give him a hard time and he would go *b-b-b-b-b-bow wow!*

—Woody Allen

*A dog, I have always said, is prose;
a cat is a poem.*

—JEAN BURDEN

Dogs are the first to recognize the superiority of cats. Their frustration is expressed in belligerence that often spells doom for the dog. No dog can handle a full-grown cat by itself. The cat will run, of course, but only until it decides how to dispose of the dog.

Tuffy, a cat of my acquaintance, used to handle its pursuers by leading them at top speed from broad daylight into my darkened garage. There Tuffy would immediately leap to the window sill and perch while the disoriented dog bounded off to stumble over lawn mowers, garbage cans and, on good days, straight into a brick wall.

—ROBERT STEARNS

I have added a romantic inmate to my family—a large bloodhound, allowed to be the finest dog of the kind in Scotland, perfectly gentle, affectionate, good-natured, and the darling of all the children. He is between the deer-greyhound and mastiff, with a shaggy mane like a lion, and always sits beside me at dinner, his head high as the back of my chair; yet it will gratify you to know that a favorite cat keeps him in the greatest possible order, insists upon all rights of precedence, and scratches with impunity the nose of an animal who would make no bones of a wolf, and pulls down a red deer without fear or difficulty. I heard my friend set up some most piteous howls (and I assure you the noise was no joke), all occasioned by his fear of passing Puss, who had stationed himself on the stairs.

—SIR WALTER SCOTT

The cat is mighty dignified until the dog comes by.

—SOUTHERN FOLK SAYING

The gingham dog went "Bow-wow-wow!"
And the calico cat replied "Me-ow!"
And the air was littered, an hour or so,
With bits of gingham and calico.

—Eugene Field

It came about by chance that a pup, a very few days old, was sent to the house by a friend, and that the gift of a kitten, whose surprised blue eyes had not long been opened, was received at nearly the same time.... Kittie and pup slept together in one bed, fed from the same saucer and plate, and their whole time when they were not sleeping was spent in play.

—W. H. Hudson

The Trouble with Cats

Cats have intercepted my footsteps at the ankle for so long that my gait, both at home and on tour, has been compared to that of a man wading through low surf.

—ROY BLOUNT, JR.

> To the pussy we're indebted
> For upholstered chairs all shredded,
> For that all-pervading stink
> For the box beneath the sink.
>
> —WILLIAM COLE

At night he sleeps sprawled at the foot of my bed, where he snores reassuringly until about five in the morning. That's when he gets cuddly: with white paw—claws retracted—he pats my face until I open my eyes. The fact that I then throw him out and slam the door in his face doesn't bother him.

—CATHRYN JAKOBSON

Cats find malicious amusement in doing what they know they are not wanted to do, and that with an affectation of innocence that materially aggravates their deliberate offense.   —HELEN WINSLOW

No favor can win gratitude from a cat.   —LA FONTAINE

That cat! I wish she were dead! But I can't shorten her days, because, you see, my poor, dear wee dog liked her. Well, there she is! And as long as she attends to Mr. C. at his meals (and she doesn't care a sheaf of tobacco for him at any other time), so long will Mr. C. continue to give her bits of meat and driblets of milk, to the ruination of carpets and hearthrugs! I have over and over again pointed out to him the stains she has made, but he won't believe them her doings.... So what I wish is that you would shut up the poor creature when Mr. C. has breakfast, dinner or tea; and if he remarks on her absence, say it was my express wish.
—JANE WELSH CARLYLE, IN A LETTER TO HER HOUSEKEEPER

The trouble with cats is that they've got no tact.
                              —P. G. WODEHOUSE

Strange Encounters

At about 4 o'clock in the morning, I was awakened. Something was treading—leisurely, thoughtfully and determinedly
—on a part of me never before trod upon. A street lamp
shone into the room and was reflected by two great blue disembodied coals burning at me. It was the cat; his claws were
unsheathed, and I arose with strangled cries of pain. I know
that the *castrato* once had his place in opera, but that was
centuries ago.   —GILBERT MILLSTEIN

In the midst of dinner, my mistress's favorite cat leaped
into her lap. I heard a noise behind me like that of a dozen
stocking weavers at work. Turning my head, I found it pro-
ceeded from the purring of this animal, who seemed to be
three times larger than an ox, as I computed by the view of
her head, and one of her paws, while her mistress was feeding and stroking her. The fierceness of this creature's countenance altogether discomposed me; though I stood at the
farther end of the table, above fifty feet off, and although
my mistress held her fast for fear she might give a spring

and seize me in her talons. But it happened there was no danger; for the cat took not the least notice of me when my master placed me within three yards of her. And as I have been always told, and found true by experience in my travels, that flying or displaying fear before a fierce animal is a certain way to make it pursue or attack you, so I resolved in this dangerous juncture to show no manner of concern. I walked with intrepidity five or six times before the very head of the cat, and came within half a yard of her; whereupon she drew herself back, as if she were more afraid of me.　　　　　　　　　　　　　　　—JONATHAN SWIFT

Eternal and Mysterious Cat

There stands before you, grey like all the other greys but one whom you won't confuse, having seen her once, with any other grey cat, she who rejects the names of queens, the childish diminutives, and is called—as if she were the only one in the world—Cat. —COLETTE

> I am the cat of cats. I am
> The everlasting cat!
> Cunning, and old, and sleek as jam,
> The everlasting cat!
> I hunt the vermin in the night—
> The everlasting cat!
> For I see best without the light—
> The everlasting cat!
>
> —ANONYMOUS

Like those great sphinxes lounging through eternity in noble attitudes upon the desert sand, they gaze incuriously at nothing, calm and wise. —CHARLES BAUDELAIRE

The animal which the Egyptians worshipped as divine, which the Romans venerated as a symbol of liberty, which Europeans in the ignorant Middle Ages anathematized as an agent of demonology, has displayed to all ages two closely blended characteristics—courage and self-respect.... The cat of the slums and alleys, starved, outcast, harried, still keeps amid the prowlings of its adversity the bold, free, panther-tread with which it paced of yore the temple courts of Thebes, still displays the self-reliant watchfulness which man has never taught it to lay aside.   —S*AKI*

> She had green eyes, that excellent seer,
> And little peaks to either ear.
> She sat there, and I sat here.
> She spoke of Egypt, and a white
> Temple, against enormous night.
> She smiled with clicking teeth and said
> That the dead were never dead;
> She said old emperors hung like bats
> In barns at night, or ran like rats—
> But empresses came back as cats!
>   —S*TEPHEN* V*INCENT* B*ENET*

The wondrous changeful luminous eye of the Cat is the reason for much of the adoration it has received. The ancient

Greek historian, Horapollon, who saw an analogy between the eye of the cat and the sun, tells us "that the cat was adored in the Temple of the Sun at Heliopolis, because the pupil of this animal follows in its proportions the height of the sun above the horizon, and in this respect resembles the marvellous planet."   —W. OLDFIELD HOWEY

Throughout history the cat has travelled. With the good commercial relations existing between Asia and Europe, cats were traded for silk in China. Cats were introduced to Japan from China in the Middle Ages. According to legend, the first cats appeared in Japan in the year 999 in the Imperial Palace of Tokyo.

—BILL PETERSEN AND JUDY FLEMING-PETERSON

The Cat is the symbol of Good and of Evil, of Light and of Darkness, of Christ and of Satan, of Religion and of Black Magic, of Sun and of Moon, of Father, Mother, and Son.

—W. OLDFIELD HOWEY

A cat sat quaintly by the fire
And watched the burning coals
And watched the little flames aspire
Like small decrepit souls.
Queer little fire with coals so fat
And crooked flames that rise,
No queerer than the little cat
With fire in its eyes.

—PEGGY BACON

Cat,
You are a strange creature.
You sit on your haunches
And yawn,
But when you leap
I can almost hear the whine
Of a released string,
And I look to see its flaccid shaking
In the place whence you sprang.

—AMY LOWELL

Dynasties of cats, as numerous as the dynasties of the
Pharoahs, succeeded each other under my roof.

—THÉOPHILE GAUTIER

Dear creature by the fire a-purr,
Strange idol, eminently bland,
Miraculous puss! As o'er your fur
I trail a negligible hand.
And gaze into your gazing eyes,
And wonder in a demi-dream
What mystery it is that lies
Behind those slits that glare and gleam.

—LYTTON STRACHEY

It seems that when man has considered himself to be the
master of all things, the cat has been shunned and feared,
being visible evidence that man could not control everything. On the other hand, when man acknowledged the
power of unknown and mysterious forces, then the cat was
respected and accepted as an equal. —H. L. COOKE

My cats are compromised. I do not entirely trust them—
they may be spies, like dolphins, reporting to some unknown authority. —JAN MORRIS

The cat is cryptic, and close to strange things which men
cannot see. —H. P. LOVECRAFT

The thing about cats,
As you may find,
Is that no one knows
What they have in mind.
—John Ciardi

There is no answer to most questions about the cat. She has kept herself wrapped in mystery for some 3,000 years, and there's no use trying to solve her now.

—Virginia Roderick

The cat in repose forms a circle, even as the serpent's head finds and bites its tail again. Thus it is the ideograph of Divinity in Nature, the Eternal, the Universal, the Complete. It is Om, the sacred Name, the prayer that exceeds all prayer and obviates words in realisation.

—W. Oldfield Howey

Though such things may appear to carry an air of fiction with them, it may be depended on that the pupils of her eyes seem to fill up and grow large upon the full of the moon and to decrease again and diminish in brightness on its waning.

—Plutarch

Who can tell what just criticisms Murr the cat may be passing on us beings of wider speculation?   —GEORGE ELIOT

"All right," said the [Cheshire] Cat; and this time it vanished quite slowly, beginning with the end of the tail, and ending with the grin, which remained some time after the rest of it had gone.   —LEWIS CARROLL

Witches and Cats

Everyone is aware that a perfectly comfortable, well-fed cat will occasionally come to his house and settle there, deserting a family by whom it is lamented, and to whom it could find its way back with ease. This conduct is a mystery which may lead us to infer that cats form a great secret society, and that they come and go in pursuance of some policy connected with education, or perhaps with witchcraft.

—ANDREW LANG

A wicked old crone
Who lived all alone
In a hut beside the reeds
With a high crowned hat
And a black tom-cat,
Whose looks were as black
   as her deeds.
—ANONYMOUS

The familiars of Witches do most ordinarily appear in the shape of cats ... this beast is dangerous in soul and body.

—EDWARD TOPSELL

Cats are a mysterious kind of folk. There is more passing in their minds than we are aware of. It comes no doubt from their being too familiar with warlocks and witches.

—SIR WALTER SCOTT

It always gives me a shiver when I see a cat seeing what I can't see.   —ELEANOR FARJEON

It is in their eyes that their magic resides.

—ARTHUR SYMONS

Its baby innocence is yet unseared. The evil knowledge of uncanny things which is the dark inheritance of cathood has not yet shadowed its round infant eyes. Where did witches find the mysterious beasts that sat motionless by their fires, and watched unblinkingly the waxen manikins dwindling in the flame? They never reared these companions of their solitude, for no witch could have endured to see a kitten gamboling on their hearthstone. A witch's kitten! That one preposterous thought proves how wide, how unfathomed, is the gap between feline infancy and age.

—AGNES REPPLIER

Cats as Omens

A cat on the doorstep in the morning brings bad luck.
—NORWEGIAN PROVERB

A cat sneezing is a good omen for everyone who hears it.
—ITALIAN PROVERB

A strange black cat on your porch brings prosperity.
—SCOTTISH PROVERB

If a black cat makes its home with you, you will have good luck.
—ENGLISH PROVERB

If a cat cross his path he will not proceed on his way.
—THEOPHRASTUS

It is bad luck to see a white cat at night.

—American proverb

Kiss the black cat,
And that'll make ye fat:
Kiss ye the white one
And that'll make ye lean

—Sir John Denham

To kill a cat brings seventeen years of bad luck.

—Irish proverb

To see a white cat on the road is lucky.

—American proverb

When the pupil of a cat's eye broadens, there will be rain.
—WELSH PROVERB

Whenever the cat of the house is black, the lasses of lovers
will have no lack. —ENGLISH FOLK SAYING

If with her tail puss played in frolic mood,
Herself pursuing, by herself pursued;
"See!" cried my nurse, "she bids for rain
  prepare,"
A storm, be sure, is gathering in the air;
If near the fire the kitten's back is found,
Frost was at hand, and snows hung hovering
    round;
Her paw prophetic rais'd above her ear
Foretold a visit, for some friend was near.
—REV. SAMUEL BISHOP

If cats desert a house, illness will always reign there.
—PROVERB

Cats and the Weather

"It's going to freeze," she would say, "the cat's dancing."
—COLETTE

> Careful observers may foretell the hour
> (By sure prognostics) when to dread a shower;
> While rain depends, the pensive cat give o'er
> Her frolics, and pursues her tail no more.
> —JONATHAN SWIFT

If the newspapers foretold a thaw, my mother would shrug her shoulders and laugh scornfully. "A thaw? Those Paris meteorologists can't teach me anything about that! Look at the cat's paws!" Feeling chill, the cat had indeed folded her paws out of sight beneath her, and shut her eyes tight. "When there's only going to be a short spell of cold," went on Sido, "the cat rolls herself into a turban with her nose against the root of her tail. But when it's going to be really bitter, she tucks in the pads of her front paws and rolls them up like a muff." —COLETTE

True calendars, as Pusses eare
Washt o're, to tell what change is neare.
— ROBERT HERRICK

She useth therefore to wash with her feet, which she
licketh and moisteneth with her tongue; and it is observed
by some that if she put her feet beyond the crown of her
head in this kind of washing, it is a sign of rain.
— JOHN SWAN

It is with the approach of winter that cats become in a special manner our friends and guests. It is then too that they
wear their richest fur and assume an air of sumptuous and
delightful opulence.   — PIERRE LOTI

*If he had asked to have the door opened,
and was eager to go out, he always went
out deliberately. I can see him now,
standing on the sill, looking about the
sky as if he was thinking whether it were*

*worth while to take an umbrella, until he
was near to having his tail shut in.*

—Charles Dudley Warner

The Spiritual Cat

He was sitting in front of the door. It is a known fact that if one sits long enough in front of the door, doing the proper yoga exercises, the door will open. —MAY SARTON

Of all animals, he alone attains the Contemplative Life. He regards the wheel of existence from without, like a Buddha. —ANDREW LANG

Sometimes he sits at your feet looking into your face with an expression so gentle and caressing that the depth of his gaze startles you. Who can believe that there is no soul behind those luminous eyes! —THÉOPHILE GAUTIER

The cat has too much spirit to have no heart.

—ERNEST MENAULT

The Cat Observed

If a fish is the movement of water embodied, given shape,
then cat is a diagram and pattern of subtle air.
>   —DORIS LESSING

> Cats, no less liquid than their shadows,
> Offer no angles to the wind.
> They slip, diminished, neat, through loopholes
> Less than themselves.
>   —A. S. J. TESSIMOND

A black cat dropped soundlessly from a high wall, like a
spoonful of dark treacle, and melted under a gate.
>   —ELIZABETH LEMARCHAND

> *Oh, the cats in this town have their
> secrets.*
>   —MARY VIRGINIA MICKA

A cat's heart is normally excited.   —COLETTE

Cat: One Hell of a nice animal, frequently mistaken for a meatloaf.   —B. KLIBAN

*N*othing's more playful
than a young cat,
nor more grave than
an old one.

                    —THOMAS FULLER

Some pussies' coats are yellow;
Some amber streaked with dark,
No member of the feline race but has a special mark.
This one has feet with hoarfrost tipped;
That one has tail that curls;
Another's inky hide is striped;
Another's decked with pearls.

                    —ANONYMOUS

Proof that cats are people:

And I say to Mr. Webster, "Mr. Webster, what are the common terms used to designate a domestic feline whose Christian name chances to be unknown to the speaker?" and Mr. Webster answers without a moment's hesitation:

"Cat, puss, pussy and pussy-cat."

"And what is the grammatical definition of the above terms?"

"They are called nouns."

"And what, Mr. Webster, is the accepted definition of a noun?"

"A noun is the name of a person, place or thing."

"Kindly define the word 'place'."

"A particular locality."

"And 'thing'."

"An inanimate object."

"That will do, Mr. Webster."

So, according to Mr. Noah Webster, the entity for which the noun 'cat' stands, must, if not a person, be a locality or an inanimate object!

A cat is surely not a locality, and as for being an inanimate object, her chance of avoiding such a condition is nine times better even than a king's. Then a cat *must* be a person.
                                                        —Oliver Herford

Nothing's more determined than a cat on a hot tin roof—is there? Is there, baby? —TENNESSEE WILLIAMS

The love of dress is very marked in this attractive animal. He is proud of the lustre of his coat, and cannot endure that a hair of it shall lie the wrong way. —JULES CHAMPFLEURY

The cat is a dilettante in fur.
—THÉOPHILE GAUTIER

A cat is a snake in furs. —EDITH WHARTON

The cat is never vulgar. —CARL VAN VECHTEN

What astonished him was that cats should have two holes cut in their coat exactly at the place where their eyes were. —GEORG CHRISTOPH LICHTENBERG

A recent census taken among cats shows that approximately one hundred percent are neurotic. That estimate is probably on the low side. —STEPHEN BAKER

The cat, if you but singe her tabby skin,
The chimney keeps, and sits content within:
But once grown sleek, will from her corner run;
Sport with her tail and wanton in the sun:
She licks her fair round face, and frisks abroad
To show her fur, and to be catterwaw'd.
        —Alexander Pope

The ideal of calm exists in a sitting cat.
        —Jules Reynard

Polar Bear did not like change. He was, when you came right down to it, a very Republican cat—he did not like anything to happen which had not happened before.
        —Cleveland Amory

One reason Garfield is interesting for cat lovers is that he confirms what they've always suspected about cats. In Garfield they see his human aspects—his refusal to diet, his inability to walk through a room without knocking things over, and his total pursuit of warm places to curl up and sleep. He champions a lot of unpopular causes, like anti-jogging, and what's more he doesn't apologize for them.

—JIM DAVIS

*O*dd *things animals. All dogs look up to you. All cats look down to you. Only a pig looks at you as an equal.*

—WINSTON CHURCHILL

One reason we admire cats is for their proficiency in one-upmanship. They always seem to come out on top, no matter what they are doing—or pretend they do.

—BARBARA WEBSTER

The cat is, above all things, a dramatist.

—MARGARET BENSEN

She scratched the flat skull which he stretched up against her hand, and the half-bald temples which showed bluish between the sparse black hairs. A tremendous purring rose from his thick neck with its white patch under the chin. The Long-cat loved no one but my mother, followed no one but her and looked to her for everything. If I took him in my arms he would imperceptibly glide out of them as though he were melting away. Except for the ritual battles and during the brief seasons of love-making, the Long-cat was nothing but silence, sleep and nonchalant night-prowlings.

—COLETTE

How cheerfully he seems to grin,
How neatly spreads his claws,
And welcomes little fishes in
With gently smiling jaws!

—LEWIS CARROLL

The cat has a nervous ear, that turns this way
    and that
And what the cat may hear, is known but to the
    cat.

—DAVID MORTON

A cat's growl is a fearsome affair. It is so unexpected. It is as if a dog, in a moment of great stress, miaowed. And Lama's growl was like a rolling crescendo of bass drums.

—DEREK TANGYE

Disturbed, the cat
Lifts its belly
Onto its back.
　　　　　—Karai Senryu

A cat's got her own opinion of human beings. She don't say
much, but you can tell enough to make you anxious not to
hear the whole of it.　　　　　—Jerome K. Jerome

There are no ordinary cats.
　　　　　—Colette

Even a cat is a lion in her own lair.   —Indian proverb

I never knew a moral cat.   —Jack Smith

Cats can be cooperative when something feels good, which, to a cat, is the way everything is supposed to feel as much of the time as possible.   —Roger A. Caras

A cat's a cat and that's that.   —American folk saying

Tail of the Cat

Cats talk with their tails.
                                    —CLEVELAND AMORY

A cat sprang up upon the bench, stretched herself, tucked her hind legs under her and coiled her tail tightly round them as though to prevent them from accidentally working loose.   —DOROTHY L. SAYERS

The tail in cats is the principal organ of emotional expression.
—ALDOUS HUXLEY

The tail, of course, must come forward until it reaches the front paws. Only an inexperienced kitten would let it dangle.
—LLOYD ALEXANDER

What a monstrous tail our cat hath got! —HENRY CAREY

Cat Tricks

Any self-respecting cat can, for example, leap some seven times or more his height. —CLEVELAND AMORY

Milena can do all kinds of tricks. She can tear a paper towel into shreds and strew it over the apartment. She can stand on her hind legs and turn on the lamp. It's the truth.

—PHILLIP LOPATE

And such a mess! All the time her cat is prowling the living room and smashing Christmas-tree balls that were not packed away because watching her belt them to smithereens is "the cutest thing." The cutest thing of all, of course, is when she has cuffed one into the bedroom and in leaping out of bed at night, I come down on it with a bare foot.

—MAYNARD GOOD STODDARD

Cats can be very funny, and have the oddest ways of show-
ing they're glad to see you. Rudimace always peed in our
shoes.   —W. H. AUDEN

Everyone with experience with cats knows how skillful
they are at jumping on to tables and mantelpieces crowded
with odds and ends, even though they cannot see them
when they begin their jump. Charles had no such skill. Every jump he made was fraught with danger to property, and
after he had knocked over sundry pieces of valuable glass
and china I had to put everything breakable out of his
reach. And he was ridiculously proud of his ability to knock
things over, to judge by the satisfied expression on his
funny little face. Only when a pile of books nearly cascaded
on top of him as a result of his efforts to dislodge them did
he show any sign of dismay. After two subdued minutes behind the curtain he was at his tricks again.

                                        —MICHAEL JOSEPH

I had a nefarious old cat, Gyp, who used to open the cup-
board door and eat any biscuits accessible. Gyp had a stroke
of paralysis, and believed he was going to die. He was in a
fright: Mr. Horace Hutchinson observed him and said that
this cat justly entertained the most Calvinistic apprehen-
sions of his future reward. Gyp was nursed back to health,

as was proved when we found him on the roof of an out-house with a cold chicken in his possession. Nothing could be more human. —ANDREW LANG

He liked to peep into the refrigerator and risked having his head shut in by closing the door. He also climbed to the top of the stove, discontinuing the practice after he singed his tail.

—LLOYD ALEXANDER

I myself thought up many games. One was trying to leap from the edge of the kitchen eaves to the roof of the main house; another was to stand on all four legs on the plum-blossom-shaped tile ends of the roof. I also tried to walk along the bamboo laundry pole (this I could not do because it is so slippery), and to jump suddenly up on a child's back from behind. This last mentioned game was more fun than

any other sport but I usually received a terrible scolding so
I try it only about three times a month at the most.

—Soseki Natsume

I'm not saying a cat won't joke. One morning I came downstairs to find a whole, perfect, upright rabbit's head on the
floor. It looked as though a rabbit had stuck its head up
through the floor to take a look around. Only the head
wasn't moving.

"Waughh!" was my first reaction. Then I realized that a
perky-looking disembodied rabbit's head on the floor was
Snope's or Eloise's idea of a joke.   —Roy Blount, Jr.

Oh, a cat's a cat. Babou's only too long when he really wants
to be. Are we even sure he's black? He's probably white in
snowy weather, dark blue at night, and red when he goes to
steal strawberries. He's very light when he lies on your
knees, and very heavy when I carry him into the kitchen in
the evenings to prevent him from sleeping on my bed. I
think he's too much of a vegetarian to be a real cat.

—Colette

One of the things I liked best about his position on my
shoulder was that it didn't ever seem to occur to him that

he couldn't just push me out of the way or take up whatever space he wanted to take up. That's where he wanted to
be, so that's where he belonged. And I had to agree. It only
seemed fair. He was little; he was being lugged around not
by his own choosing; he had no idea where he was going or
why. If he wanted to sit somewhere and at least get a good
view, how could I complain? I felt—and I think this is one
of those clever things that cats somehow manage to do—
honored by the fact that he chose me to be his piece of furniture. —PETER GETHERS

The head moves slowly back and forth, eyes wide, looking
for the perfect spot. The moment is right and Penguin
launches herself on to the bookcase. Papers fly and books
fall over, but that doesn't matter, because for some reason
known only to her, she had to be precisely there at that
moment. —BILL FLEMING AND JUDY PETERSON-FLEMING

There is something going on now in Mexico that I happen
to think is cruelty to animals. What I'm talking about, of
course, is cat juggling. —STEVE MARTIN

They are quiet only at night. To give them a sense of security, of belonging, I treated them to crimson cushions to

sleep on, but it didn't work; they sleep on me. When I lie on
my left side, they sleep along the ridges formed by my arm,
hip and thigh; when I roll over, they take to treading me. If
I bend down to pick up something, they leap onto my back
and crouch there, beginning a leisurely bath. When I re-
ceive guests, they scale forbidden bookshelves before my
eyes and swat houseplants. They once ate two ferns and
shredded my terry-cloth robe. When I bark a command—
"Heel!"—they collapse, roll over, and squirm with delight.
When I stand quite still and look down at them in blank despair, they wind themselves about my ankles and croon and
have no other gods before me. They hear things that cannot
really be heard. But as watchdogs they are a total flop.

—KATINKA LOESER

What he would do, once I was in the tub, was to jump up
on the edge of the tub—a precarious leap, considering his
game hip—balance himself, and then make a slow solemn
trip around. He would start first toward the back of the
tub, stopping at each point when he got to my shoulders.
Here he would lean toward me, give me a head nudge and
a small nip, and then proceed on. When he got to the business end of the tub, he would carefully investigate the
spout, and, if I had not turned it on just enough for him to

drink a few drops, he would turn and tell me to do so. And, of course, I would. —CLEVELAND AMORY

Where food was concerned Charles, like all cats, was an incorrigible thief.... On one occasion he disgraced us by stealing a cold roast chicken from the house opposite. —MICHAEL JOSEPH

This white cat would drive me insane if I had to live in the same apartment with it under my feet, rubbing against my leg, rolling on its back in front of me, leaping up on the table to paw at the typewriter. He's on top of the TV, he's pawing the telephone. —WILLIAM S. BURROUGHS

Substance Abuse

My cat has taken to mulled port and rum punch.
Poor old dear! He is all the better for it.

—JEROME K. JEROME

Catnip is vodka and whisky to most cats.

—CARL VAN VECHTEN

Webster sat crouched upon the floor beside the widening pool of whisky. But it was not horror and disgust that had caused him to crouch. He was crouched because, crouching, he could get nearer to the stuff and obtain crisper action. His tongue was moving in and out like a piston.

—P. G. WODEHOUSE

'Twas that reviving herb, that Spicy Weed,
The Cat-Nip. Tho' tis good in time of need,
Ah, feed upon it lightly, for who knows
To what unlovely antics it may lead.

—OLIVER HERFORD

Love of Cats

A morning kiss, a discreet touch of his nose landing somewhere on the middle of my face. Because his long white whiskers tickled, I began every day laughing.

—JANET F. FAURE

A cat stretches from one end of my childhood to the other.

—BLAGA DIMITROVA

Come, lovely cat, and rest upon my heart,
And let my gaze dive in the cold
Live pools of thine enchanted eyes that dart
Metallic rays of green and gold.

—CHARLES BAUDELAIRE

Everybody thinks that *their* cats are the best. They don't feel that way about anything else—they don't think their wives or their cars or even their dogs are the best—but they all think their cats are just terrific. Amazing product, cats. And real simple to manufacture.

—MICHAEL O'DONOGHUE

Here as elsewhere the old rule generally holds good: the men love their dogs; the women, their cats.

—ELIZABETH COATSWORTH

How could anyone prefer, I have frequently asked myself, the bare bony form of a human, male or female, to the perfection of a feline, whether thrillingly predatory in the shape of a cheetah, or voluptuously tantalizing in that of my own preference, an Abyssinian cat?   —JAN MORRIS

I can say with sincerity that I like cats. A cat is an animal which has more human feeling than almost any other.

—EMILY BRONTË

I love cats because I love my home, and little by little they become its visible soul. A kind of active silence emanates from these furry beasts who appear deaf to orders, to appeals, to reproaches and who move in a completely royal authority through the network of our acts, retaining only those which intrigue them or comfort them.

—JEAN COCTEAU

I have found my love of cats most helpful in understanding women.

—JOHN SIMON

I love cats. I love their grace and their elegance. I love their independence and their arrogance, and the way they lie and look at you, summing you up, surely to your detriment, with that unnerving, unwinking, appraising stare.

—JOYCE STRANGER

I would like to be there, were it but to see how the cat jumps. —SIR WALTER SCOTT

In the matter of animals I love only cats, but I love them unreasonably for their qualities and in spite of their numerous faults. I have only one, but I could not live without a cat. —J. K. HUYSMANS

It is impossible for a lover of cats to banish these alert, gentle, and discriminating friends, who give us just enough of their regard and complaisance to make us hunger for more. —AGNES REPPLIER

Most judges are cat lovers. —CARL VAN VECHTEN

Often he would sit looking at me, and then, moved by a delicate affection, come and pull my coat and sleeve until he could touch my face with his nose, and then go away contented. —CHARLES DUDLEY WARNER

Pluto—this was the cat's name—was my favorite pet and playmate. I alone fed him, and he attended me wherever I

went about the house. It was even with difficulty that I could prevent him from following me through the streets.
—Edgar Allan Poe

Those who early loved in vain
Use the cat to try again,
And test their bruised omnipotence
Against the cat's austere defense.
—Edward N. Horn

She [the cat] hasn't had her full ration of kisses-on-the-lips today. She had the quarter-to-twelve one in the Bois, she had the two o'clock one after coffee, she had the half-past-six one in the garden, but she's missed tonight's. —Colette

Squid, for all her play acting, is a lover. She often does such intense figure eights around our ankles it becomes all but impossible to walk, and that not just when she wants food, either. She appears from nowhere when you are trying to read or watch television and jumps into your lap or climbs up onto your shoulders to drape herself to sleep there. You wake up and find out that she has been sharing your pillow.
—Roger A. Caras

The more I see of people, the more I love my cat.

                                    —BUMPER STICKER

There were a total of four cats. Twelve years ago, my wife bought the first one, Noko Marie, for three dollars. We kept one male, Norton, from the first litter. And we kept Nitty from the second batch. Nitty was my favorite—a big, fat, striped cat. Then some little kids gave my wife a stray we named Burton Rustle. As a kid, I used to hate them because I was violently allergic, but I loved those four cats. One day Norton just disappeared. It almost broke my heart. Nitty got feline leukemia and died in my arms—that did break my heart.   —B. KLIBAN

Those who love cats which do not even purr,
Or which are thin and tired and very old,
Bend down to them in the street and stroke
    their fur
And rub their ears and smooth their breast, and
    hold
Their paws, and gaze into their eyes of gold.
                                    —FRANCIS SCARFE

The difference between Papa and Mamma is that Mamma
loves morals and Papa loves cats.

—SUSY CLEMENS (MARK TWAIN'S DAUGHTER)

*They did not love him for his glossy
tiger coat, nor for his great green eyes,
no, not even for the white tip to his tail.
They loved him because he was himself.*

—MAY SARTON

To understand the character of a cat, to respect her independence, to recognize and deplore her pitiless instincts, to
be charmed by her gentler moods, to admire her beauty, to
appreciate her intelligence, and to love her steadfastly
without being loved in return—these things are not often
possible to the Anglo-Saxon nature.

—AGNES REPPLIER

What does it mean to love an animal, a pet, in my case a
cat, in the fierce, entire and unambivalent way that some of

us do? I really want to know this. Does the cat (did the cat) represent some person, a parent or a child? some part of one's self? I don't think so—and none of the words or phrases that one uses for human connections sounds quite right: "crazy about," "really liked," "very fond of"—none of those describes how I felt and still feel about my cat.

—ALICE ADAMS

> I like little Pussy, her coat is so warm;
> And if I don't hurt her she'll do me no harm.
>
> —JANE TAYLOR

I shall never forget the indulgence with which he treated Hodge, his cat; for whome he himself used to go out and buy oysters, lest the servants having that trouble should take a dislike to the poor creature. I am, unluckily, one of those who have an antipathy to a cat, so that I am uneasy when in the room with one; and I own, I frequently suffered a good deal from the presence of the same Hodge.

I recollect him one day scrambling up Dr. Johnson's breast, apparently with much satisfaction, while my friend, smiling and half-whistling, rubbed down his back, and pulled him by the tail; and when I observed he was a fine cat, saying, "Why, yes, Sir, but I have had cats whom I liked better than this"; and then, as if perceiving Hodge to be out of countenance, adding, "but he is a very fine cat, a very fine cat indeed."   —James Boswell

A charm of cats is that they seem to live in a world of their own, just as much as if it were a real dimension of space.

—Harriet Prescott Spofford

Lots and Lots of Cats

As I was going to St. Ives,
I met a man with seven wives,
Each wife had seven sacks,
Each sack had seven cats,
Each cat had seven kits:
Kits, cats, sacks, wives,
How many were going to St. Ives?

—NURSERY RHYME

The big kitchen–living room had been completely given over to cats. There were cats on the sofas and chairs and spilling in cascades on to the floor, cats sitting in rows along the window sills and, right in the middle of it all, little Mr. Bond, pallid, wispy-mustached, in his shirt sleeves reading a newspaper.

—JAMES HERRIOT

The white tower had been built by Mary in an effort to get the complement of thirty cats out of the house, and to provide Ernest [Hemingway] with a place more becoming to work in than his bedroom. It worked with the cats but not with Ernest. The ground floor of the tower was the cats' quarters, with special sleeping, eating and maternity accommodations, and they all lived there with the exception of a few favorites like Crazy Christian, Friendless' Brother and Ecstasy, who were allowed house privileges.

—A. E. HOTCHNER

With Richelieu the taste for cats was a mania; when he rose in the morning and when he went to bed at night he was always surrounded by a dozen of them with which he played, delighting to watch them jump and gambol. He had one of his chambers fitted up as a cattery, which was entrusted to overseers, the names of whom are known. Abel and Teyssandier came, morning and evening, to feed the cats with *patés* fashioned of the white meat of chicken.

—ALEXANDRE LANDRIN

Jeanne Toomey has 446 cats! (Yes, four hundred and forty-six.)

That means her household contains 1,784 paws, 446 elegant and eloquent tails, 892 pointed but fuzzy ears and enough feline nonchalance to float an ark.

—ANDREW H. MALCOLM

Cat People

"Cat People," when we discover one another either by confession or the telltale presence of cat hairs upon their clothing, are apt to rush hysterically into one another's arms with little shrieks of joy, embrace like long-lost relatives and recognize immediately that they are set apart from other mortals. Or they will instantly retire from the middle of any gathering off to a corner to exchange anecdotes. The attitude is one of having found a fraternity brother or sorority sister, one more member of the elite outstanding in a world of Yahoos. Dearly beloved friends and fellow cat lovers, I notice to my distress that we are becoming self-congratulatory and standing in the greatest peril of becoming a group of thundering bores.   —PAUL GALLICO

There is, incidentally, no way of talking about cats that enables one to come off as a sane person.

—DAN GREENBURG

Cat people are different, to the extent that they generally are not conformists. How could they be, with a cat running their lives?   —Dr. Louis J. Camuti

At Trewellard, for instance, there was a huge tabby sitting on a garden wall, sitting peacefully, eyes half closed, when he was suddenly awoken from his dreams by Beverley and Jeannie jumping out of the car, hastening towards him with arms outstretched, and cooing those curious noises which are peculiar to cat worshippers. The tabby, however, I have to admit enjoyed it.   —Derek Tangye

But thousands die without or this or that,
Die, and endow a college or a cat.
          —Alexander Pope

I would never wound a cat's feelings, no matter how downright aggressive I might be to humans.

          —A. L. Rowse

It often happens that a man is more humanely related to a cat or dog than to any human being.

—HENRY DAVID THOREAU

To be reminded that one is very much like other members of the animal kingdom is often funny ... though ... I do not too much mind being somewhat like a cat.

—JOSEPH WOOD KRUTCH

When cat people get together they are as single-minded as vegetarians, or kelp and soybean addicts. For they can talk for hours about what their cats will and will not eat. Once you meet a cat lover you will pursue his or her cat's food predilections endlessly.

—GLADYS TABOR

The Company of Cats

The cat is the companion of the fireside.

—EDWARD E. WHITING

Mistletoe hung from the gas in all the front parlours; there was sherry and walnuts and bottled beer and crackers by the dessertspoons; and cats in their fur-abouts watched the fires; and the high-heaped fires crackled and spat, all ready for the chestnuts and the mulling pokers.

—DYLAN THOMAS

Whene'er I felt my towering fancy fail,
I stroked her head, her ears, her tail,
And, as I stroked, improved my dying song
From the sweet notes of her melodious tongue.
Her purrs and mews so evenly kept time,
She purred in metre and she mewed in rhyme.

—JOSEPH GREEN

There are two means of refuge from the miseries of life: music and cats.

—ALBERT SCHWEITZER

But once gain his confidence, and he is a friend for life. He shares your hours of work, of solitude, of melancholy. He spends whole evenings on your knee, purring and dozing, content with your silence, and spurning for your sake the society of his kind. —THÉOPHILE GAUTIER

For me, one of the pleasures of cats' company is their devotion to bodily comfort.

—COMPTON MACKENZIE

And close beside me the cat sits purring,
Warming her paws at the cheery gleam;
The flames keep flitting, and flicking, and
    whirring;
My mind is wrapped in a realm of dream.
                                    —HEINRICH HEINE

When I'm discouraged, he's empathy incarnate, purring and
rubbing to telegraph his dismay.   —CATHRYN JAKOBSON

How many times have I rested tired eyes on her graceful
little body, curled up in a ball and wrapped round with her
tail like a parcel. . . . If they are content, their contentment
is absolute; and our jaded wearied spirits find a natural relief in the sight of creatures whose little cups of happiness
can be so easily filled to the brim.   —AGNES REPPLIER

Lily, our Siamese, keeps an eye on the robins at the far end
of the garden but accompanies me as I make the rounds.
She wants to be fed. If hungry, she rubs against my legs. If
the situation is desperate, she stands on my feet. Lily
spends much time with me in the garden, occasionally taking off on some private cat business and turning up as ab-
ruptly as she vanished.   —WILLIAM LONGGOOD

She would walk up and down between the beds [of daffodils], the black plume of her tail mingling with the green spikes of the daffodil leaves; and sometimes when I was bending down to pick a stem, she would come to me, pushing her head against my hand, and then I would cease to pick, and proceed to pay her the attention she expected of me. Or I would put a basket down at the edge of a meadow, go on with my picking, then look back and find her sitting in the basket.   —DEREK TANGYE

When Paderewski made his concert debut at St. James's Theatre in London, he was terrified as he approached the piano, observing the audience staring fixedly at him. As he settled in to play his first number, a cat that lived in the theater jumped into his lap. This so delighted the audience and so charmed and calmed the brilliant young composer and pianist that he allowed the cat to remain there purring throughout the opening etude. Until his dying day Paderewski swore that the cat got him over the first hurdle.   —ROGER A. CARAS

She soon turned into a rather portly cat whose pale yellow eyes became hot pools of luminescent greens when she met my headlights late at night. Almost from the beginning she displayed an even temper. She made her way through dogs

and children with unruffled dignity. She washed both sides
of her face with her left paw, and when I scratched the spot
at the base of her spine that she couldn't reach herself, she
lifted her face in ecstasy and stuck out her tongue.

—Irving Townsend

*My mother thought it would make us
feel better to know animals had no souls
and thus their deaths were not to be
taken seriously. But it didn't help and
when I think of some of the animals I've
known, I wonder. The only really
"soulful" eyes in the world belong to the*

*dog or cat who sits on your lap or at
your feet commiserating when you cry.*
                                        —LIZ SMITH

The boon companion of the colossal elephant was a common
cat! This cat had a fashion of climbing up the elephant's
hind legs, and roosting on his back. She would sit up there,
with her paws curved under her breast, and sleep in the
sun half the afternoon. It used to annoy the elephant at first
and he would reach up and take her down, but she would go
aft and climb up again. She persisted until she finally conquered the elephant's prejudices, and now they are insepa-
rable friends.   —MARK TWAIN

The cat, like many other animals, will often form singular
attachments. One would sit in my horse's manger and purr
and rub against his nose, which undoubtedly the horse enjoyed, for he would frequently turn his head purposely to
be so treated. One went as consort with a Dorking cock; another took a great liking to my collie, Rover; another loved
Lina, the cow; while another would cosset up close to a sitting hen, and allowed the fresh-hatched chickens to seek
warmth by creeping under her.   —HARRISON WEIR

The Owl and the Pussy-cat went to sea
In a beautiful pea-green boat:
They took some honey, and plenty of money
Wrapped up in a five-pound note.
The Owl looked up to the stars above,
And sang to a small guitar,
'O lovely Pussy, O Pussy, my love,
What a beautiful Pussy you are,
You are,
You are!
What a beautiful Pussy you are!'

—EDWARD LEAR

There is something about the presence of a cat ... that seems to take the bite out of being alone.

—DR. LOUIS J. CAMUTI

Comfortable Cats

A cat knows how to be comfortable, how to get the people around it to serve it. In a tranquil domestic situation, the cat is a veritable manipulative genius. It seeks the soft, it seeks the warm, it prefers the quiet and it loves to be full. It displays, when it gets its own way in these matters, a degree of contentment we would all like to emulate. If we could relax like a cat we would probably live at least a hundred and twenty-five years, and then we could relax to death. Cats know how not to get ulcers. We may seek that level of tranquillity, but we seldom achieve it.

—ROGER A. CARAS

Cats at fireside live luxuriously and are the picture of comfort.

—LEIGH HUNT

He confined himself to the parsley bed which the she-cat let him have, and there he would sprawl, warming his long belly, with its withered teats, in the sun. Or else he would drape himself over the heap of firewood, as if the spiky faggots were wool and down. For a cat's idea of what is comfortable is not comprehensible to a human.   —Colette

The most unsociable cat, when it finds itself wrapped up in someone's coat and put to sleep upon his bed—stroked, fed and tended with every imaginable care—soon ceases to stand upon its dignity.   —Murasaki Shikibu

There are people who reshape the world by force or argument, but the cat just lies there, dozing, and the world quietly reshapes itself to suit his comfort and convenience.
          —Allen and Ivy Dodd

You could never accuse him of idleness, and yet he knew the secret of repose.   —Charles Dudley Warner

If there is one spot of sun spilling onto the floor, a cat will find it and soak it up.
          —Joan Asper McIntosh

Playing Cats

There is nothing in the animal world, to my mind, more delightful than grown cats at play. They are so swift and light and graceful, so subtle and designing, and yet so richly comic.   —MONICA EDWARDS

How she beggeth, playeth, leapeth, looketh, catcheth, tosseth with her foot, riseth up to strings held over her head, sometimes creeping, sometimes lying on the back, playing with one foot ...   —EDWARD TOPSELL

One of them likes to be crammed into a corner-pocket of the billiard table—which he fits as snugly as does a finger in a glove and then he watches the game (and obstructs it) by the hour, and spoils many a shot by putting out his paw and changing the direction of a passing ball. Whenever a ball is in his arms, or so close to him that it cannot be played upon with risk of hurting him, the player is privileged to remove it to one of the 3 spots that chances to be vacant.
     —SAMUEL L. CLEMENS, IN A LETTER

Although all cat games have their rules and ritual, these vary with the individual player. The cat, of course, never breaks a rule. If it does not follow precedent, that simply means it has created a new rule and it is up to you to learn it quickly if you want the game to continue.

—SIDNEY DENHAM

Cats are notoriously sore losers. Coming in second best, especially to someone as poorly coordinated as a human being, grates their sensibility.   —STEPHEN BAKER

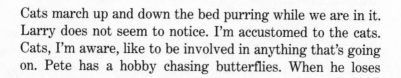

Cats do not need to be shown how to have a good time, for they are unfailingly ingenious in that respect.

—JAMES MASON

Cats march up and down the bed purring while we are in it. Larry does not seem to notice. I'm accustomed to the cats. Cats, I'm aware, like to be involved in anything that's going on. Pete has a hobby chasing butterflies. When he loses sight of one, he searches the air, wailing pathetically, as though abandoned. Brenda plays with paper clips. She likes the way she can hook a paper clip so simply with one claw. She attacks spiders in the same way. Their legs draw up and she drops them.   —BOBBIE ANN MASON

We entertain each other with mutual follies, and if I have my time to begin or to refuse, she also has hers.

—MICHEL DE MONTAIGNE

Those who play with cats must expect to be scratched.

—CERVANTES

Purring Cats

It is a very inconvenient habit of kittens ... that, whatever you say to them, they always purr.   —LEWIS CARROLL

When the tea is brought at five o'clock,
And all the neat curtains are drawn with care,
The little black cat with bright green eyes
Is suddenly purring there.

—HAROLD MONRO

Even if you have just destroyed a Ming vase, purr. Usually all will be forgiven.

—LENNY RUBENSTEIN

"Four" has the best purr I have ever known, bar none, a purr with a quite astonishing vocal range. If he were not called "Four" I should call him "Callas," because his purr really has a prima donna quality.   —BEVERLEY NICHOLS

A cat can be trusted to purr when she is pleased, which is more than can be said for human beings.

—WILLIAM INGE

A typical cat quirk is that they can purr. We don't pretend to know what kind of mechanism goes into the making of a purr, or how to wind it up once it runs down. However, this much is known: There are a wide variety of purrs which range from the almost inaudible to the kind which can be felt through the floor. Loud purring might possibly set up sympathetic vibrations in a building and send it crashing to the ground. For these reasons, as well as others too numerous to mention, lions make very poor household pets.

—ERIC GURNEY

But in the morning Chuck purrs against my throat, and it feels like prayer.   —AMY HEMPEL

Cats use their voices much as a means of expression, and they utter under various emotions and desires at least six or seven different sounds. The purr of satisfaction which is made during both inspiration and expiration, is one of the most curious.   —CHARLES DARWIN

> Her conscious tail her joy declared,
> The fair round face, the snowy beard,
> The velvet of her paws,
> Her coat, that with the tortoise views,
> Her ears of jet, and emerald eyes,
> She saw; and purr'd applause.
>   —THOMAS GRAY

His purr, when he purred for sheer happiness of life, was as the purr of many kettles.   —OSWALD BARRON

If we treated everyone we meet with the same affection we bestow upon our favorite cat, they, too, would purr.
                              —MARTIN BUXBAUM

My own preference was for the midnight unsolicited purr. For the first years, until we found a fox waiting for Monty to jump out, he had the freedom of the window at night. He used to go in and out and we were never disturbed if he chose to spend the night outside, perhaps in the barn. But when he did choose to remain indoors, and instead of settling on the sofa, preferred a corner of our bed, we felt flattered. It was then that I have relished, when sometimes I lay awake, the rich, rolling tones of an unsolicited purr.

—DEREK TANGYE

Purring would seem to be, in her case, an automatic safety-valve device for dealing with happiness overflow.

—MONICA EDWARDS

The purr is an indescribable sound, and this forced combination of letters, namely "prrrrrr," does it no justice. One can only refer to the sense of joy and tranquillity experienced by the purrer and transferred to the soul of the listener. There are times, though regrettably not too many, when we ourselves would purr if we could. Yet, with all our faculties, we simply have no way of expressing our completest satisfaction with the moment to compare with that of House Cat.   —PAUL GALLICO

There was a sound between them. A warm and contented sound like the murmur of giant bees in a hollow tree.
                              —STEPHEN VINCENT BENET

There were the unsolicited purrs. A cat has to be in a very bad mood if a human cannot coax him to purr. There is little honor in this achievement, only the satisfaction that a minute or two is being soothed by such a pleasant sound. But the unsolicited purrs belong to quite another category. These are the jewels of the cat fraternity, distributed sparingly, like high honors in a kingdom. They are brought about by the great general contentment. No special incident induces them. No memory of past or prospect of future banquets. Just a whole series of happy thoughts suddenly combine together and whoever is near enough is lucky enough to hear the result. Thus did Monty from time to time reward us. —DEREK TANGYE

For he purrs in thankfulness, when God tells him he's a good cat.

—CHRISTOPHER SMART

Louder he purrs and louder,
In one glad hymn of praise
For all the night's adventures,
For quiet, restful days.

Life will go on forever,
With all that cat can wish;
Warmth, and the glad procession
Of fish and milk and fish.

Only—the thought disturbs him—
He's noticed once or twice,
That times are somehow breeding
A nimbler race of mice.

—SIR ALEXANDER GRAY

Rubbing himself against my cheek he purred like the kettle-drums in Berlioz's *Requiem.* —C*ARL* V*AN* V*ECHTEN*

It was difficult to feel vexed by a creature that burst into a chorus of purring as soon as I spoke to him.

—P*HILIP* B*ROWN*

Though speech he had not, and the unpleasant kind of utterance given to his race he would not use, he had a mighty power of purr to express his measureless content with congenial society. There was in him a musical organ with stops of varied power and expression, upon which I have no doubt he could have performed Scarlatti's celebrated cat's fugue. —C*HARLES* D*UDLEY* W*ARNER*

To please himself only the cat purrs. —I*RISH PROVERB*

*To err is human
To purr feline.*

—R*OBERT* B*YRNE*

Sleeping Cats

Cats everywhere asleep on the shelves like motorized bookends. —AUDREY THOMAS

One of the ways in which cats show happiness is by sleeping. —CLEVELAND AMORY

A cat sleeps fat, yet walks thin. —FRED SCHWAB

A little drowsing cat is an image of perfect beatitude. —JULES CHAMPFLEURY

A sleeping cat is ever alert.
—FRED SCHWAB

All cats sleep an amazing amount—close to three-quarters of the time, I would estimate, counting, of course, the kind of nap which they have made famous. —Cleveland Amory

Average number of hours a person sleeps each night: 7.5
Average number of hours a cat sleeps: 14.8
—The Better Sleep Council

Cats are rather delicate creatures and they are subject to a good many ailments, but I never heard of one who suffered from insomnia. —Joseph Wood Krutch

Cats will always lie soft.
—Theocritus

Drowsing, they take the noble attitude of a great sphinx, who, in a desert land, sleeps always, dreaming dreams that have no end. —Charles Baudelaire

He and I were standing inside the threshold of his bare country room and bending over a box where the mother cat was sleeping with her four kittens. The children were all sleeping head to foot, with their tails in each other's mouths so that together they looked like one big cat.

—PHILLIP LOPATE

He loved books, and when he found one open on the table he would lie down on it, turn over the edges of the leaves with his paw, and, after a while, fall asleep, for all the world as if he had been reading a fashionable novel.

—THÉOPHILE GAUTIER

I wish you could see the two cats drowsing side by side in a Victorian nursing chair, their paws, their ears, their tails complementally adjusted, their blue eyes blinking open on a single thought of when I shall remember it's their suppertime. They might have been composed by Bach for two flutes. —SYLVIA TOWNSEND WARNER

If left to their own devices, felines tend to nap and nibble throughout the day and night, scarcely differentiating between the two. —LYNN HOLLYN

In my experience, cats and beds seem to be a natural combination.

—Dr. Louis J. Camuti

Kittens are born with their eyes shut. They open them in about six days, take a look around, then close them again for the better part of their natural lives. —Stephen Baker

Purring in his sleep, Fletch stretches out his little black paws to touch my hands, the claws withdrawn, just a gentle touch to assure him that I am there beside him as he sleeps.   —William S. Burroughs

The friendship of the two cats for each other grew stronger in such close companionship. In the depth of an armchair, or on their cushions before the fire, they slept for days together, rolled up into one big furry ball, without visible head or tail. —Pierre Loti

The yellow cat ... is dreaming. His paws twitch now and then, and once he makes a small, suppressed remark with his mouth shut. I wonder what a cat dreams of, and to whom he was speaking just then. —Ursula K. Le Guin

Let sleeping cats lie.

—French proverb

Losing a Cat

The Ancient Egyptians went into mourning for the loss of a cat and shaved their eyebrows. And why shouldn't the loss of a cat be as poignant and heartfelt as any loss? Small deaths are the saddest, sad as the death of monkeys.

—WILLIAM S. BURROUGHS

Bathsheba:
To whom none ever said scat,
No worthier cat
Ever sat on a mat
Or caught a rat:
    Requies-cat.

—JOHN GREENLEAF WHITTIER

Because a man is higher up on the evolutionary scale than the cat doesn't necessarily mean that a man's death is more painful for those he leaves than for those who have lost a cat. Should one mourn more for an indifferent uncle than for a devoted and loving pet? It would be a strange person who did so.   —DR. LOUIS J. CAMUTI

Dear little ghost, whose memory has never faded from my heart.... Sleep sweetly in the fields of asphodel, and waken, as of old, to stretch thy languid length, and purr thy soft contentment to the skies.   —AGNES REPPLIER

He purred when I stroked him. If he was really ill he was making no fuss or complaint. An hour later I carried him downstairs to give him his pill, and then I saw that he was worse. He lay listlessly in my arms, and the lightness of him frightened me. He seemed to have lost weight very suddenly.

I put him gently down on a cushion in front of the fire and he began to cough silently, his tongue hanging out. I hurried to get a kettle of boiling water for the friar's balsam. When I returned a few minutes later he was behind the curtains of the French windows. I picked him up and he lay still in my arms, his jaw sagging. As gently as I could, I put him in his basket, which I had put on a chair over the steaming kettle. He rose feebly to his feet, turned round twice, and laid down as if to sleep. But I knew it was no ordinary sleep. My little cat was dead.   —MICHAEL JOSEPH

Heathcliff's death shocked my cats as much as it did me. Janine wept for the old faker and I confess I did the same. At my worktable, I sat alone—with the feeling of disagreeable lightness that comes when a cat just left your lap. Seeing his box in the corner, and a few tangled strings about the floor, I half expected Heathcliff himself to arrive at any moment. But, rationally, I knew I should never see my old friend again. For my remaining tigers, it was a more difficult matter. This time, I felt that the boundary between their world and mine had never been drawn so sharply. My cats could not ask me what had happened and it was impossible for me to tell them. They would somehow have to understand in their own way. I could not share the human faculty of resignation.   —LLOYD ALEXANDER

> Housemate, I can think you still
> Bounding to the window-sill,
> Over which I vaguely see
> Your small mound beneath the tree,
> Showing in the autumn shade
> That you moulder where you played.
>   —THOMAS HARDY

I had only one cat, and he was more a companion than a cat. When he departed this life I did not care to, as many men do when their partners die, take a second.

—CHARLES DUDLEY WARNER

I miss Ed more for his acts of mischief than his endearing moments. Yesterday I had bought cat food. (Ed has been missing now for about twenty-four hours. No, more like forty-eight now. We got back from Paris on Friday the thirteenth and he had just slipped away two hours before that.)

I used to put the cans of cat food on the window sill over the sink and Ed would get up on the sill and knock the cans down into the sink. A terrible clatter would wake me up. What have you done now, Ed? A broken dish, a glass knocked to the floor and broken ... So I started to put the cans into the cabinet, where he wouldn't have access. Now, as I am taking the cat food out of my shopping bag, I look at the sill and think, Well, I can put the cans up there now. And at this moment I feel a sharp pang of loss, the loss of a loved presence, however small. —WILLIAM S. BURROUGHS

No heaven will not ever Heaven be
Unless my cats are there to welcome me.

—EPITAPH

Pet was never mourned as you,
Purrer of the spotless hue,
Plumy tail and wistful gaze,
While you humoured our queer ways,
Or outshrilled your morning call
Up the stairs and through the hall—
Foot suspended in its fall—
While, expectant, you would stand
Arched, to meet the stroking hand;
Till your way you chose to wend
Yonder, to your tragic end.

—Thomas Hardy

Suppose a cat died a natural death under a family roof. The inhabitants of the house shaved their eyebrows and lamented loudly for hours. The eyes of the beloved deceased were piously closed. The whiskers were firmly pressed down against its lips. And then it was wound round with a mummy's wrappings.... Depending on how rich its masters were, it was either buried or placed in a true sarcophagus.

—Fernand Méry

There is nothing more touching than a sick animal; it submits to suffering with such gentle, pathetic resignation.

Everything possible was done to try to save Pierrot. He

had a very clever doctor who sounded him and felt his pulse. He ordered him asses' milk, which the poor creature drank willingly enough out of his china saucer. He lay for hours on my knee like the ghost of a sphinx, and I could feel the bones of his spine like the beads of a rosary under my fingers. He tried to respond to my caresses with a feeble purr which was like a death rattle.

When he was dying he lay panting on his side, but with a supreme effort he raised himself and came to me with dilated eyes in which there was a look of intense supplication. This look seemed to say: "Cannot you save me, you who are a man?" Then he staggered a short way with eyes already glazing, and fell down with such a lamentable cry, so full of despair and anguish, that I was pierced with silent horror.

—THÉOPHILE GAUTIER

*T*he beautiful cat endures and endures.

—GRAVE INSCRIPTION (THEBES)

Who shall tell the lady's grief
When her cat was past relief?
Who shall number the hot tears
Shed o'er her, belov'd for years?
Who shall say the dark dismay
Which her dying caused that day?

Of a noble race she came,
And Grimalkin was her name.
Young and old full many a mouse
Felt the prowess of her house;
Weak and strong full many a rat
Cowered beneath her crushing pat;
And the birds around the place
Shrank from her too-close embrace.
But one night, reft of her strength,
She lay down and died at length:
Lay a kitten by her side
In whose life the mother died.
Spare her life and lineage,
Guard her kitten's tender age,
And that kitten's name as wide
Shall be known as hers that died.
And whoever passes by
The poor grave where Puss doth lie,
Softly, softly let him tread,
Nor disturb her narrow bed.

—CHRISTINA ROSSETTI

Whenever he was out of luck and a little down-hearted, he would fall to mourning over the loss of a wonderful cat he used to own (for where women and children are not, men of kindly impulses take up with pets, for they must love something). And he always spoke of the strange sagacity of that cat with the air of a man who believed in his secret heart that there was something human about it—maybe even supernatural.
                                                        —MARK TWAIN

Learning from Cats

Cat lessons are there for everybody, you only have to love and ask—not what you want to know but what it is they would like you to know.　　　　　—ANITRA FRAZIER

Cats are intended to teach us that not everything in nature has a function.　　　　　—GARRISON KEILLOR

Cats, incidentally, are a great warm-up for a successful marriage—they teach you your place in the household.
　　　　　—PAUL GALLICO

I am indebted to the species of the cat for a particular kind of honorable deceit, for a great control over myself, for characteristic aversion to brutal sounds, and for the need to keep silent for long periods of time.　　　　　—COLETTE

In these days of tension, human beings can learn a great deal about relaxation from watching a cat, who doesn't just lie down when it is time to rest, but pours his body on the floor and rests in every nerve and muscle.

—Murray Robinson

There is, indeed, no single quality of the cat that man could not emulate to his advantage. —Carl Van Vechten

You can't look at a sleeping cat and be tense.

—Jane Pauley

But so control your actions that
Your friends may all repeat,
"This child is dainty as the Cat,
And as the Owl discreet."
                    —Hilaire Belloc

If men and women would become more feline, indeed, I think it would prove the salvation of the human race.
                    —Carl Van Vechten

To Be a Cat!

It is better, under certain circumstances, to be a cat than to be a duchess . . . no duchess of the realm ever had more faithful retainers or half so abject subjects.

—HELEN WINSLOW

As Gertrude Stevens awoke one morning from uneasy dreams, she found herself transformed in her bed into a plump orange cat. When she lifted her head, she could see a long striped tail gracefully arched at the top. Her skin had become soft and furlike, and, beneath her eyes, whiskers protruded.

—RONI SCHOTTER

I think it would be great to be a cat! You come and go as you please. People always feed and pet you. They don't expect much of you. You can play with them, and when you've had enough, you go away. You can pick and choose who you want to be around. You can't ask for more than that.

—PATRICIA MCPHERSON

No one can have experienced to the fullest the true sense of achievement and satisfaction who has never pursued and successfully caught his tail.   —ROSALIND WELCHER

Taffy, the topaz-coloured cat,
Thinks now of this and now of that,
But chiefly of his meals.
Asparagus, and cream, and fish,
Are objects of his Freudian wish;
What you don't give, he steals.

His amiable amber eyes
Are very friendly, very wise;
Like Buddha, grave and fat,
He sits, regardless of applause,
And thinking, as he kneads his paws,
What fun to be a cat!
        —CHRISTOPHER MORLEY

The Mouse should stand in Feare,
So should the squeaking Rat;
All this would I doe if I were
Converted to a Cat.
        —GEORGE TURBERVILLE

Rules for Cats

No animal should ever jump up on the dining-room furniture unless absolutely certain he can hold his own in the conversation. —FRAN LEBOWITZ

The problem of cat versus bird is as old as time. If we attempt to resolve it by legislation, who knows but what we may be called upon to take sides as well in the age-old problems of dog versus worm.... The State of Illinois and its local governing bodies already have enough to do without trying to control feline delinquency. —ADLAI STEVENSON

 When human folk at table eat
A kitten must not mew for meat,
Or jump to grab it from a dish
(Unless it happens to be fish).
  —OLIVER HERFORD

Cat's-Eye View

Waking up owners:

The purpose is to get the owner out of bed, with no reprisals, to feed you or pet you. A closeup technique is the best: select an ear and purr into it continually; or, use the wet nose approach, gently tapping the human's ear, nose or cheek with your nose. This is especially effective with soft-hearted humans; avoid using with violent types.

—LENNY RUBENSTEIN

When you see your person settle down to do some fireside or after-dinner reading, jump up into his or her lap, get comfortable, and then put your paws across the book or paper. This will make turning the pages difficult, and after a while you will find they will give up.   —PAUL GALLICO

In a cat's eyes, all things belong to cats.
—ENGLISH PROVERB

The real objection to the great majority of cats is their insufferable air of superiority. Cats, as class, have never completely got over the snootiness caused by the fact that in Ancient Egypt they were worshipped as gods. This makes them too prone to set themselves up as critics and censors of the frail and erring human beings whose lot they share. They stare rebukingly. They view with concern. And on a sensitive man this often has the worst effect, inducing an inferiority complex of the gravest kind. —P. G. WODEHOUSE

Marcia was washing the breakfast dishes when she first heard her cat thinking. I'm thirsty, why doesn't she give me more water, there's dried food on the sides of my bowl. There was a pause. I wonder how she catches the food. She can't stalk anything, she always scares the birds away. She never catches any when I'm nearby. Why does she put it into those squares and round things when she just has to take it out again? —PAMELA SARGENT

Whether or not you wish to take over the bed is entirely up to you, and here again you will find yourself involved in that astonishing ambivalence that seems to be part of people and that never ceases to surprise me, even while I welcome it. They won't want you on the bed, and at the same time, they *will* want you on the bed. If this is a paradox it is because that is what people seem to be like. . . .

But to return to the bed, the point is they can't have it both ways. It either is or it isn't your territory, and since they can't make up their minds, it is up to you to make up yours. If you prefer the bed to your own box or chair for sleeping, establish this immediately. The chances are they will be flattered and think that it is because you can't bear to be away from them, and they will use it as a brag: "Our cat always sleeps at the foot of the bed," to which, if you like, you can get them to add, "And comes and wakes us in the morning," by simply getting up when you have had enough sleep and walking across their faces, which they seem to enjoy.   —Paul Gallico

Do you see that kitten chasing so prettily her own tail? If you could look with her eyes, you might see her surrounded with hundreds of figures performing complex dramas, with tragic and comic issues, long conversations, many characters, many ups and downs of fate.

—Ralph Waldo Emerson

Then my Man lifts me up and buries his warm face in my fur. Just then, for a second a flash of higher existence awakens in him, and he sighs with bliss and purrs something which is almost understandable.　—KAREL CAPEK

Cats consider theft a game,
And howsoever you may blame,
Refuse the slightest sign of shame.

—ANONYMOUS

I was then two years old, and was at the same time the fattest and most naïve cat in existence. At that tender age I still had all the presumptuousness of an animal who is disdainful of the sweetness of home.

How fortunate I was, indeed, that providence had placed me with your aunt! That good woman adored me. I had at the bottom of a wardrobe a veritable sleeping salon, with feather cushions and triple covers. My food was equally excellent; never just bread, or soup, but always meat, carefully chosen meat.

Well, in the midst of all this opulence, I had only one desire, one dream, and that was to slip out of the upper window and escape on the roofs. Caresses annoyed me, the softness of my bed nauseated me, and I was so fat that it was disgusting even to myself. In short, I was bored the whole day long just with being happy.   —EMILE ZOLA

Oh I am a cat that likes to
Gallop about doing good.
                    —STEVIE SMITH

I wonder what goes through his mind when he sees us peeing in his water bowl.   —PENNY WARD MOSER

Cat Talk

Hamlet found the Algonquin surpassingly mnrhnh. Cats speak a subtle language in which few sounds carry many meanings, depending on how they are sung and purred. Mnrhnh means comfortable soft chairs. It also means dark aged wood, admiration, permanence, and the absence of dogs. It means fertile for dreams.　　—VAL SCHAFFNER

We cats are all capable of talking, had we not acquired from human beings a contempt for speech.　　—LUDWIG TIECK

If a cat spoke, it would say things like, "Hey, I don't see the problem here."

　　　　　　　　　　　　　　　　—ROY BLOUNT, JR.

Ignorant people think it's the noise which fighting cats make that is so aggravating, but it ain't so; it's the sickening grammar they use.　　—MARK TWAIN

"What can that cat want?" I said to myself. "She has had her dinner. She is not hungry. What is she after?"

In answer to my unspoken question, la Chinoise crept nearer and nearer until she could touch my foot. Then sitting upright, with her tail curled close about her, she uttered a gentle little cry, gazing meanwhile straight into my eyes, which seemed to hold some message she could read. She understood that I was a thinking creature, capable of pity, and accessible to such mute and piteous prayer; and that my eyes were mirrors in which her anxious little soul must study my good or bad intentions. It is terrifying to think how near an animal comes to us, when it is capable of such intercourse as this.   —Pierre Loti

An outrageous cat, more outrageous even than most cats are. She is sometimes passionately affectionate; she will press her fine-boned body against Maggie's leg, or her shoulder, with purrings and rubbings. But at other times, which are wholly of Diana's choosing, she can be haughty, even cross; she has a large vocabulary of negative sounds, as well as her loud, round purr.   —Alice Adams

Cats have a contempt of speech. Why should they talk when they can communicate without words?
                    —Lilian Jackson Braun

And he lifts his voice, and wildly
Sings an old cat-battle song,
That, like far-off thunder rolling,
Sweeps the storm-vexed night along.

Never a child of man can hear it—
Each sleeps heedless in his house;
But, deep down in darkest cellar,
Hears, and paling, quakes the mouse.

—Josef Victor von Scheffel

Doubtless cats talk and reason with one another.

—Izaak Walton

Even in Europe the cat's cry is "meow."

—Ceylonese proverb

Far in the stillness a cat languishes loudly.

—W. E. Henley

His advances were subtle: a movement of the head, a light grazing of our legs with his flank, a glance, a moment of purring. Unobvious things that we gradually learned to observe and interpret. The nearest Rabbit came to effusiveness was rolling—his specialty. He would sink down in a long, slow glide until his head touched the floor, then deftly throw himself over on his back, wiggling his hind paws in a supreme gesture of good will. But a cat usually writes his love notes in shorthand and reading them demands a certain amount of practice.

—Lloyd Alexander

His voice is tenderly discreet;
But let it be serene or vexed
Still always it is sonorous and profound,
This is his charm and his secret.

—Charles Baudelaire

If you speak cat at all there is no reason why you should not speak it fluently. It is simply a matter of application.
—SYLVIA TOWNSEND WARNER

Once when she was in heat, I lost patience with her constant "come-and-get-me" yelling. In irritation, I found myself yelling back at her in exact imitation. This turned out to be just what the little witch wanted, and it delighted her beyond measure.
—WINIFRED CARRIERE

She claws at the window, meows and looks beseechingly at me where I sit reading.... When I come to the window she no longer meows with sound. Only the mouth opens in a silent imploring prayer.
—LIV ULLMANN

She whurleth with her voice, having as many tunes as turnes, for she hath one voice to beg and complain, another to testifie her delight and pleasure, another among her own kind ... in so much as some have thought that [cats] have a peculiar intelligible language among themselves.
—EDWARD TOPSELL

Slowly, with a look of intense concentration, he got up and advanced on me ... put out a front paw, and stroked my cheek as I used to stroke his chops. A human caress from a cat. I felt very meager and ill-educated that I could not purr. —Sylvia Townsend Warner

You opened the door for her if she crossed the room and gave you a look. She made you know what she meant as if she had the gift of speech. —Sarah Orne Jewett

A cat that lives with a good family is used to being talked to all the time.

—Lettice Cooper

Cats and Their People

People make great companions for cats because they practically take care of themselves.... All a cat has to do is purr and rub against their legs every now and then and they're content. I get such a kick out of watching humans play, too—when they're running around in the morning late for work, when they're ripping through stacks of bills.

—MORRIS THE CAT

Of all the toys available, none is better designed than the owner himself. A large multipurpose plaything, its parts can be made to move in almost any direction. It comes completely assembled and it makes a sound when you jump on it.

—STEPHEN BAKER

Every cat knows that the ideal housekeeper is an old maid, if possible living in a small house with a garden. The house should have both an attic and a cellar, the attic for fun and games, the cellar for hunting.

—MAY SARTON

Nobody who is not prepared to spoil cats will get from them the reward they are able to give to those who do spoil them.   —COMPTON MACKENZIE

She wants her breakfast at a certain hour in the morning; if the door of my bedroom is closed she gives little cries outside. If it is open she enters, puts her forepaws on the edge of my bed close to my face and licks my cheek. If I brush her away, in a few moments she is nibbling my toes. I put an end to this and very shortly she is marching up and down, using me as a highroad. She is equally persistent if I am taking a nap. On such occasions she often climbs high on my chest and sleeps with me, but when she awakes she digs her claws into my chest and stretches, quite as if I didn't exist. This alternate protrusion of the forepaws, with toes separated, as if pushing against and sucking their mother's teats, is a favourite gesture of cats when they are pleased.
                          —CARL VAN VECHTEN

Any normal, ordinary cat can keep any human being in a state of frustration.
                          —GLADYS TABOR

At dinner time they would sit in a corner, concentrating, and suddenly they would say, "Time to feed the cat," as if it were their own idea.   —LILIAN JACKSON BRAUN

Bless their little pointed faces and their big, loyal hearts. If a cat did not put a firm paw down now and then, how could his human remain possessed?   —WINIFRED CARRIERE

Cats love one so much more than they will allow. But they have so much wisdom they keep it to themselves.
—MARY E. WILKINS FREEMAN

He shut his eyes while Saha [the cat] kept vigil, watching all the invisible signs that hover over sleeping human beings when the light is put out.   —COLETTE

I have noticed that what cats most appreciate in a human being is not the ability to produce food which they take for granted—but his or her entertainment value.
—GEOFFREY HOUSEHOLD

If I called her she would pretend not to hear, but would come a few moments later when it could appear that she had thought of doing so first.

—ARTHUR WEIGALL

My cat does not talk as respectfully to me as I do to her.

—COLETTE

Somebody once said that a dog looked up to a man as its superior, that a horse regarded a man as its equal, and that a cat looked down on him as its inferior.

—COMPTON MACKENZIE

Sometimes the veil between human and animal intelligence wears very thin—then one experiences the supreme thrill of keeping a cat, or perhaps allowing oneself to be owned by a cat.   —CATHERINE MANLEY

Sometimes when the two cats were on the bed, one on either side of her, she would lie in the dark and stroke both of them, marveling at the peculiar sensuality of her life.
                                                             —ROBLEY WILSON, JR.

The cat is the mirror of his human's mind, personality and attitude, just as the dog mirrors his human's physical appearance.
                                                            —WINIFRED CARRIERE

There is a fable, Chinese I think, literary I am sure: of a period on earth when the dominant creatures were cats: who after ages of trying with the anguishes of mortality—famine, plague, war, injustice, folly, greed—in a word, civilized government—convened a congress of the wisest cat philosophers to see if anything could be done: who after long deliberation agreed that the dilemma, the problems themselves were insoluble and the only practical solution was to give it up, relinquish, abdicate, by selecting from among the lesser creatures a species, a race optimistic enough to believe that the mortal predicament could be solved and ignorant enough never to learn better. Which is why the cat lives with you, is completely dependent on you for food and shelter but lifts no paw for you and loves you not; in a word, why your cat looks at you the way it does.

—William Faulkner

There is nothing so lowering to one's self-esteem as the affectionate contempt of a beloved cat.　　—Agnes Repplier

To a cat, human beings are an inferior, servile race, always to be kept in their places, with occasional rewards if they perform well. To love a cat is uphill work, and therefore very rewarding.　　　　　　　　—Haskel Frankel

To a cat, we are probably not much more than a big obstacle much of the time. Cats don't bump into us unless they want a good bit of rubbing or they want to stake claim on our ankles or our dining-room chair.   —ROGER A. CARAS

To anyone who has ever been owned by a cat, it will come as no surprise that there are all sorts of things about your cat you will never, as long as you live, forget. Not the least of these is the first sight of him or her.

—CLEVELAND AMORY

Tobermory looked squarely at her for a moment and then fixed his gaze serenely on the middle distance. It was obvious that boring questions lay outside his scheme of life.

—SAKI

Whatever you do, don't treat us like dogs. We don't fetch slippers or newspapers. If you want a servant, hire a hound. If your cat rolls over and plays dead, you're in trouble. We don't need authority figures like canines do.

—MORRIS THE CAT

When my cat and I entertain each other with mutual antics, as when playing with a garter, who knows but that I make more sport for her than she makes for me?

—MICHEL DE MONTAIGNE

When a cat adopts you there is nothing to be done about it
except to put up with it and wait until the wind changes.
—T. S. Eliot

You are my cat and I am your human.
—Hilaire Belloc

Questions for Cats

Why so lean, my lady cat?
Is it fasting causes that?
Say, or is it love?
—Matsuo Basho

Do cats eat bats? ... Do bats eat cats? —Lewis Carroll

Is it enough to know that one creature likes what you do
and the way you do it and that that creature is your cat?
—Naomi Thornton

Pussy cat, pussy cat, where have you been?
I've been up to London to visit the Queen.
—Nursery rhyme

Who shall hang the bell about the cat's neck?

—CERVANTES

Understanding Cats

Never wear anything that panics the cat. —P. J. O'ROURKE

Send not a cat for lard. —GEORGE HERBERT

It doesn't do to be sentimental about cats; the best ones don't respect you for it. —SUSAN HOWATCH

Dogs are disciplined, horses are enslaved, cows and pigs are exploited. Only cats join us as opportunistic partners. They do things for us, we do things for them, and when both sides feel like it we share the pleasure of each other's company. —JAN MORRIS

Every cat I've known has had a distinct personality. Unmistakably. I've never known two cats even vaguely alike. —AMY TAUBIN

I'm not one of those as can see the cat in the dairy, and wonder what she's come after. —GEORGE ELIOT

Only a Frenchman can understand the fine and subtle qualities of the cat. —THÉOPHILE GAUTIER

To understand a cat, you must realize that he has his own gifts, his own viewpoint, even his own morality.
—LILIAN JACKSON BRAUN

We cannot, without becoming cats, perfectly understand the cat mind. —SAINT GEORGE MIVART

What sort of philosophers are we who know absolutely nothing about the origin and destiny of cats?
—HENRY DAVID THOREAU

Cats don't like change without their consent.
—ROGER A. CARAS

The Artist's Cat

Because of our willingness to accept cats as superhuman creatures, they are the ideal animals with which to work creatively.   —RONI SCHOTTER

I started drawing cats as a result of marrying into a cat-loving family. I married twenty-two years ago and received a cat education from that point on.   —GEORGE BOOTH

I've never gone in search of a cat; they always find me—in Colorado, Maine, on the Bowery. Cats are as much a part of my life as painting. After all, a cat and art are only two letters removed.   —ROBERT INDIANA

It's an honor to paint cats.
                    —OLIVER JOHNSON

Nothing is so difficult as to paint the cat's face, which as Moncrif justly observes, bears a character of "finesse and hilarity." The lines are so delicate, the eyes so strange, the movements subject to such sudden impulses, that one should be feline oneself to attempt to portray such a subject.

—Jules Champfleury

Painting cats is a question of genius. —Théophile Gautier

Perhaps it is because cats do not live by human patterns, do not fit themselves into prescribed behavior, that they are so united to creative people.

—André Norton

To respect the cat is the beginning of the aesthetic sense.

—Erasmus Darwin

Women, poets, and especially artists, like cats; delicate natures only can realize their sensitive nervous systems.

—Helen Winslow

The smallest feline is a masterpiece.

—LEONARDO DA VINCI

The Writer's Cat

We sublet to Vladimir Nabokov and his beautiful wife, Vera, and they were delighted to accept Tom Jones as a cherished paying guest during their stay. What a bonanza for a gentleman cat to be taken into such a notable family with kind Vera and Felidae-lover Vladimir! And to hear cat language translated into Russian.   —MAY SARTON

A catless writer is almost inconceivable. It's a perverse taste, really, since it would be easier to write with a herd of buffalo in the room than even one cat; they make nests in the notes and bite the end of the pen and walk on the typewriter keys.   —BARBARA HOLLAND

> A poet's cat, sedate and grave,
> As poet well could wish to have,
> Was much addicted to inquire
> For nooks, to which she might retire,
> And where, secure as mouse in chink,
> She might repose, or sit and think.

I know not where she caught the trick—
Nature perhaps herself had cast her
In such a mould philosophique,
Or else she learn'd it of her master.
                              —WILLIAM COWPER

Advice to the writer's cat:

But to return to preventing the writer from getting on with his work. As soon as he sits down at the typewriter, climb into his lap and start the game. Never wait until he has begun or becomes interested in what he is doing, for then your task will be more difficult and you might even suffer the indignity of being thrown out into the garden or shut up in the kitchen. You will learn that it is exactly at the moment when he sits down at the typewriter that he is at his weakest and can be most easily put off, for it has taken a tremendous effort for him to bring himself to the point of getting down to the machine.   —PAUL GALLICO

As an inspiration to the author, I do not think the cat can be over-estimated. He suggests so much grace, power, beauty, motion, mysticism. I do not wonder that many writers love cats; I am only surprised that all do not.
                              —CARL VAN VECHTEN

Am writing an essay on the life-history of insects and have abandoned the idea of writing on "How Cats Spend Their Time."

—W. N. P. BARBELLION

And now he is about to sleep, maybe to dream, on this table at which I am writing; he settles down as close to me as possible, after stretching out his paw towards me two or three times, looking at me as though craving permission to leap on to my knees. And there he lies, his head daintily resting on my arm, as though to say: "Since you will not have me altogether, permit me this at least, for I shall not disturb you if I remain so."   —PIERRE LOTI

Cats and monkeys, monkeys and cats—all human life is there.   —HENRY JAMES

Cats are dangerous companions for writers because cat watching is a near-perfect method of writing avoidance.
           —DAN GREENBURG

Cats speak to poets in their natural tongue, and something profound and untamed in us answers.
           —JEAN BURDEN

For a workingman like me, a cat is the perfect counterpart. After breakfast, and a brief workout to keep down his weight, he is ready for a nap at the very moment I am ready to bend to my daily task. So long as I do not rustle the papers upon my desk too ardently, or ply my electric typewriter with too fierce a fury, he is content to remain asleep, and largely invisible, until the dinner hour.

—Rogers E. M. Whitaker

He had a habit of coming into my study in the morning, sitting quietly by my side or on the table for hours, watching the pen run over the paper, occasionally swinging his tail round for a blotter, and then going to sleep among the papers by the inkstand. Or, more rarely, he would watch the writing from a perch on my shoulder. Writing always interested him, and, until he understood it, he wanted to hold the pen.

—Charles Dudley Warner

I and Pangur Ban, my cat,
'Tis a like task we are at;
Hunting mice is his delight,
Hunting words I sit all night.

—Anonymous Irish monk

I have just been called to the door by the sweet voice of Toss, whose morning proceedings are wonderful. She sleeps—She has just jumped on my lap, and her beautiful tail has made this smudge, but I have put her down again. I was going to say that she sleeps on an arm-chair before the drawing-room fire; descends the moment she hears the servants about in the morning, and makes them let her out; comes back and enters Flu's room with Eliza regularly at half-past seven. Then she comes to my door and gives a mew, and then—especially if I let her in, and go on writing or reading without taking any notice of her—there is a real demonstration of affection, such as never again occurs in the day. She purrs, she walks round and round me, she jumps in my lap, she turns to me and rubs her head and nose against my chin, she opens her mouth and raps her pretty white teeth against my pen. Then she leaps down, settles herself by the fire, and never shows any more affection all day.

                                                        —MATTHEW ARNOLD

If by chance I seated myself to write, she very slyly, very tenderly, seeking protection and caresses, would softly take her place on my knee and follow the comings and goings of my pen—sometimes effacing, with an unintentional stroke of her paw, lines of whose tenor she disapproved.

                                                        —PIERRE LOTI

In the evening she would curl up on my lap and close her eyes and make that motor-running, steady-breathing sound. I didn't have the heart to move, with her on my lap, purring like that. Moreover, she held her paw on my wrist, as if to detain me. How could I reach for my pencil?

—PHILLIP LOPATE

My theory is that the writer senses a deep and profound kinship with the cat.

—JOYCE CAROL OATES

My study at Maynard Place was at the top of the house; a small, sunny room, one wall lined with books, and on the windowed side a long trestle table and a straight chair. Nabokov removed this austere object and replaced it with a huge over-stuffed armchair where he could write half lying down. Tom Jones soon learned that he was welcome to install himself at the very heart of genius on Nabokov's chest, there to make starfish paws, purr ecstatically, and sometimes—rather painfully for the object of his pleasure—knead. I like to imagine that Lolita was being dreamed that year and that Tom Jones' presence may have had something to do with the creation of that sensuous world. At any rate, for him it was a year of grandiose meals and subtle passions.　—MAY SARTON

Sometimes when I have racked my brain
In writing sonnet or quatrain,
My Cat lies curled up in a ball,
Asleep, oblivious to all.
And then perhaps at last when I
Achieve my aim and breathe a sigh
Of gratitude, she wakes and views
Me wonderingly as if the muse
Were something she would hardly deem
As worthwhile, say—as meat or cream,
And languidly she eyes my sonnet,
Then stretches and sits down upon it.
　　　　　　　—MARGARET E. BRUNER

George Moore's cat, "the great black tom cat of Ebury Street," was the first audience to Moore's work *Avowals*. The cat sat sedately in an armchair blinking his green eyes while his master made his famous plea in defense of censored literature.

—John Hosford Hickey and Priscilla Beach

So I passed him some very good advice, that if you want to concentrate deeply on some problem, and especially some piece of writing or paper-work, you should acquire a cat. Alone with the cat in the room where you work, I explained, the cat will invariably get up on your desk and settle placidly under the desk lamp. The light from a lamp, I explained, gives a cat great satisfaction. The cat will settle down and be serene, with a serenity that passes all understanding. And the tranquillity of the cat will gradually come to affect you, sitting there at your desk, so that all the excitable qualities that impede your concentration compose themselves and give your mind back the self-command it has lost. You need not watch the cat all the time. Its presence alone is enough. The effect of a cat on your concentration is remarkable, very mysterious.

—MURIEL SPARK

INDEX

ABOUT THE EDITOR

MARIA POLUSHKIN ROBBINS is the author of twelve cookbooks and several children's books. She has edited two other quotation collections: *A Cook's Alphabet of Quotations* and *A Gardener's Bouquet of Quotations*, both from The Ecco Press. She lives with her husband in East Hampton, New York.